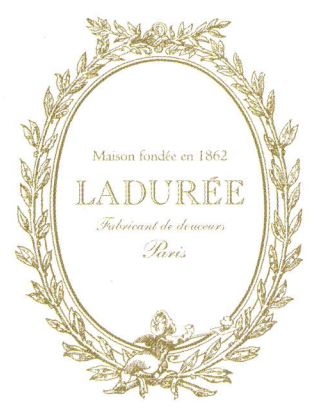

Entertaining

RECIPES, IDEAS & INSPIRATION

Entertaining
RECIPES, IDEAS & INSPIRATION

PASTRY CHEF: VINCENT LEMAINS

EXECUTIVE HEAD CHEF: MICHEL LEROUET

PHOTOGRAPHY: MARIE-PIERRE MOREL

STYLIST: MINAKO NORIMATSU

An Art to Share

· • • ·

Famed throughout the world for its peerless cuisine, France is equally unrivalled in the art of entertaining – an art that, over the centuries, has become an intrinsic part of the French national heritage.

As heirs to this tradition, we at Maison Ladurée attach a particular importance to the décor of our shops and salons de thé, devoting the same meticulous care to their presentation and ambience as we do to our mouthwatering delicacies. Honed and perfected in our establishments around the world, this *l'art de recevoir* is now envied and emulated by all those who appreciate French elegance and style.

No one is immune from those moments of panic at the thought of organizing a formal dinner, a romantic supper, or even a simple family lunch. In the past, our grandmothers would have handed down their books of recipes and household tips, treasuries of sound advice for all occasions. Today, in a world where daily life is a constant race against the clock, this volume is designed to perpetuate the inimitably French art of entertaining, restoring that *je ne sais quoi* of chic style to every event, no matter how grand or informal.

In Entertaining, we offer advice, tips and designs for settings and decorations that will enable you to host any kind of event, whether planned long in advance or casually impromptu, with faultless and impeccable confidence and style – the perfect recipe for happy, relaxed occasions brimming over with small but perfectly pitched details.

Très chic, très Ladurée …

Contents

· • • • ·

An Art to Share…
PAGE 4

BREAKFASTS
PAGE 8

BIJOU BRUNCHES
PAGE 40

CHIC PICNICS
PAGE 72

FAMILY LUNCHES
PAGE 104

AFTERNOON TEAS
PAGE 136

BUFFET SUPPERS
PAGE 168

ROMANTIC DINNERS
PAGE 200

WINTER SUPPERS
PAGE 232

FORMAL DINNERS
PAGE 264

Recipe Index
PAGE 296

Guest Book
PAGE 300

Vincent Lemains, Pastry Chef
Michel Lerouet, Executive Head Chef
PAGE 315

Breakfasts

SELFISH BREAKFAST

⋅⋅●⋅⋅

Concorde Omelette

Poached Eggs with Bacon

Herbed *Fromage Blanc* Finger Sandwiches

Melun Brie Cheese with Almonds

Apple-Rhubarb Compote

Black Fig Turnovers

⋅⋅●⋅⋅

Omelette Concorde
Concorde Omelette

Serves 1
Preparation: 20 minutes
Cook: 3 minutes

Filling
1 medium tomato
1 tbsp peeled, seeded and finely diced cucumber
2 slices cooked chicken breast
3 young spinach leaves
Salt, ground white pepper

Omelette
2 very fresh eggs
1 tbsp heavy (double) cream
1 tbsp (15 g) butter

Assembly
Fleur de sel (sea salt crystals)

Filling
1. Remove and discard the tomato stem. Prepare a bowl of ice water. Bring a saucepan of water to the boil and immerse the tomato for 10 seconds and transfer immediately to the ice water to cool; drain. Peel, quarter, seed and finely dice the tomato; set aside with the diced cucumber. Finely dice the sliced chicken breast; set aside. Stack, roll and finely slice the spinach leaves. Combine all the filling ingredients in a bowl and season with salt and pepper; set a little aside to garnish the omelette.

Omelette
2. Break the eggs into a bowl, and whisk briskly. Add the cream; season with salt and pepper. Melt the butter in a non-stick frying pan. Pour the egg mixture into the pan. Use a rubber spatula and constantly push the liquid egg mixture from the outer edge of the omelette back into the centre to cook. Turn off the burner after 30 seconds. The centre of the omelette will still be moist and will finish cooking from the residual heat.

Assembly
3. Spread the centre of the omelette with the filling. Roll up and cut it into large segments. Decorate with the reserved garnish. Sprinkle with *fleur de sel*. Serve immediately.

Chef's Tip
Heavy cream is added to the omelette to make it smooth and moist.

Œufs pochés au bacon
Poached Eggs with Bacon

Serves 1
Preparation: 15 minutes
Cook: 4 minutes

8 cups (2 L) water
4 tsp (20 ml) distilled white vinegar
1 tsp coarse salt
2 very fresh eggs
2 slices bacon
Fleur de sel (sea salt crystals)

Equipment
2 small ramekins

1. Put the water, vinegar and coarse salt into a medium, frying or sauté pan; bring to the boil. When the water comes to a rolling boil, reduce the heat until the water simmers slowly and evenly.
2. Break one egg into each ramekin. Position the ramekin just above the surface of the water. Slide the egg gently into the water. The white will wrap around the yolk and start to coagulate. Use two spoons to gather the white around the yolk to enclose it. Or, push the egg(s) carefully to the wall of the pan to seal the edges of the whites. Repeat for the second egg.

Poach until the whites are firm to the touch but not rubbery, about 4 minutes. Use a skimmer to transfer the eggs to a bowl of cold water to stop the cooking and rinse off the vinegar.

3. Cook the bacon in a non-stick pan and set aside on kitchen paper to drain.
4. Arrange the poached eggs and bacon on a warm plate. Sprinkle with *fleur de sel*. Serve immediately.

Chef's Tip
Before serving, trim off the trailing bits of egg white using a small knife. The salt plays a valid role here and is used to bring out the flavour; the vinegar is essential for coagulation of the egg whites. If desired, serve this dish with buttered toast fingers.

Fingers au fromage blanc et herbes fraîches

Herbed Fromage Blanc Finger Sandwiches

Serves 1
Preparation: 10 minutes

½ tsp sliced flat leaf parsley
½ tsp sliced chives
½ tsp sliced tarragon leaves
Salt, ground white pepper
2 tbsp (30 g) *fromage blanc* (fresh white cheese)
4 thin slices white bread, crusts removed

1. Stir the sliced herbs into the *fromage blanc*; season to taste with salt and pepper.
2. Spread the *fromage blanc* mixture evenly over two slices of the bread. Place the other two slices on top. Cut the sandwiches into rectangles. Serve immediately.

Chef's Tip

Slice the fresh herbs, do not chop them! Otherwise, your finger sandwiches will taste like cut grass. If the sandwiches are prepared in advance, wrap in wax (greaseproof) paper to keep them fresh and moist.

Brie de Melun aux amandes

Melun Brie Cheese with Almonds

Serves 1
Preparation: 10 minutes
Cook: 6 minutes
Rest: 30 minutes

2 tbsp fresh almonds, peeled
1 tbsp sliced (flaked) almonds
2 tsp grape seed oil
1 small Melun Brie cheese
4 tsp unsweetened organic almond cream

1. Preheat the oven to 320°F, 160°C or gas mark 3. Set out two small baking sheets. Put the fresh almonds on one and the flaked almonds on the other; sprinkle with the grape seed oil. Roast in the oven for 6 minutes. Set aside to cool.
2. Place the cheese flat on a work surface and cut it horizontally in halves. Spread one half with the almond cream. Put a few grilled almonds aside for decoration. Sprinkle the remainder on the almond cream and place the other cheese half on top; set aside for 30 minutes. Before serving, decorate the Melun Brie cheese with the remaining grilled almonds.

Compote pommes-rhubarbe
Apple-Rhubarb Compote

Makes 5 small jars
Preparation: 1 hour 15 minutes
Cook: 50 minutes

18 oz (500 g) rhubarb
13 oz (375 g) Boskoop apples
5 tbsp (75 g) butter
6 tbsp (75 g) granulated sugar
1 pinch cinnamon

Equipment
5 small jars

1. Wash and peel and cut the rhubarb stalks into small pieces; set aside. Peel, quarter and core the apples; set aside.
2. Melt the butter in a large saucepan, add the rhubarb, and sprinkle with the sugar. Cook over low heat for 30 minutes, stirring from time-to-time.
3. Stir in the apples and continue cooking over low heat for another 20 minutes.
When the fruit is tender, add the pinch of cinnamon. Divide the compote evenly between the jars. Eat warm or cold.

Chef's Tip
Strawberry lovers, why not prepare strawberry-rhubarb compote? Simply replace the apples with fresh strawberries. To retain all of their wonderful springtime flavour, add them at the end, just before the rhubarb is almost cooked.

Chaussons à la figue violette
Black Fig Turnovers

Order this dessert from your local Ladurée patisserie.

The Art of Entertaining

Setting the Stage

IMAGINE A SCENE WORTHY OF A 5-STAR HOTEL

Set the table. Cover it with a beautiful, white floor-length tablecloth. Put a smaller, daintier cloth over the top of it. Set out your best porcelain tableware, and the crystal glasses... Don't forget the silver cutlery and a vase containing a rose as fresh as the early morning dew. These are the details that convey style. Enjoy a breakfast fit for a king, or queen, but for you and you alone.

A Question of Style

BE LUXURIOUSLY SELF-INDULGENT

Sink lazily and pleasurably into a novel... finish it when you want, without worrying about the time or anyone else for that matter. You have a regal breakfast to accompany and keep you going.

Let yourself be carried away, perhaps to the strains of an entire Verdi opera... Contemplate the meaning of life while listening to a recorded philosophical conference...
Or, feel the emotion of a story being read by an irresistible voice...

A Touch of Folly

DO SOMETHING OUT OF THE ORDINARY

Have a superb bouquet of your favourite flowers delivered...maybe an armful of Chinese peonies... or fresh sweet peas in the middle of winter? Hire a waiter so that you do not have to lift a finger, allowing you to spend the entire time in your armchair, carefully positioned before the garden window, to watch the shadows and sunlight dancing on the lawn. Fill your apartment with the perfume of lilies or fresh jasmine...

ROMANTIC BREAKFAST

••••

Soft-Boiled Eggs with Black Truffle

Scrambled Eggs with Sea Urchin Roe

Fromage Blanc and Raspberries

French Toast with Apricot Compote

••••

Œufs mollets à la truffe noire

Soft-Boiled Eggs with Black Truffle

Serves 2
Preparation: 10 minutes
Cook: 6 minutes

---

4 very fresh eggs
¼ oz (8 g) black truffle
1 scant tsp *fleur de sel* (sea salt crystals)
1 tbsp (15 ml) extra virgin olive oil
4 tbsp (60 ml) heavy (double) cream
Salt, ground white pepper
Fleur de sel (sea salt crystals)

---

1. Put the eggs into a saucepan and cover with cold water. Bring to the boil, reduce the heat and cook for 6 minutes; drain and peel immediately. If the eggs are too hot to handle, cool in a bowl of ice water. This will make them easier to peel.
2. Finely slice the black truffle. Season the slices with the scant teaspoon of *fleur de sel* and the olive oil.
3. Reduce the cream over medium heat until slightly thickened; season to taste with salt and pepper. Set aside.
4. Warm the plates. Arrange two soft-boiled eggs on each one, decorate with sliced truffle. Drizzle with the warm cream; sprinkle with *fleur de sel*. Serve immediately.

Chef's Tip
If possible, use the black truffle (tuber melanosporum) *because it is better quality and is more perfumed than the black Chinese truffle known as* tuber ancinatum.

Œufs brouillés à l'oursin

Scrambled Eggs with Sea Urchin Roe

Serves 2
Preparation: 20 minutes
Cook: 5 minutes

Sea Urchins
6 sea urchins
3½ tbsp (50 ml) water
2 tsp (10 g) butter
Salt, ground white pepper

Scrambled Eggs
4 very fresh eggs
5 tsp (25 ml) heavy (double) cream
2 tsp (10 g) butter
Fleur de sel (sea salt crystals)

Sea Urchins

1. Hold the sea urchins over a bowl to recuperate the juice. Cut open the shells using scissors. Carefully scoop out the roe (coral) and pour any remaining juice into the bowl. Rinse the roe under gently running cold water; set aside.
2. Put a fine mesh wire strainer over a small saucepan and strain the sea urchin juice into it to remove the impurities; add the water. Bring the liquid to the boil. Remove from the heat as soon as it starts to boil. Add the 2 tsp (10 g) of butter and season to taste with salt and pepper; whisk or mix to combine. Set the sea urchin *jus* aside to keep warm.

Scrambled Eggs

3. Break the eggs into a bowl. Add 4 tsp (20 ml) of the cream and stir until all the ingredients are well combined.
4. Melt the butter in a frying pan. Pour the beaten egg mixture into the pan and cook over low heat stirring continuously with a whisk. When the scrambled eggs are cooked but still lightly liquid, remove from the heat and stir in the remaining teaspoon of cream.

Assembly

5. Divide the scrambled eggs evenly between two warm soup plates. Arrange the sea urchin roe on the eggs and spoon the reserved *jus* over the top. Sprinkle with *fleur de sel*. Serve immediately.

Chef's Tip
Sea urchins are fragile. Handle carefully and consume as soon as they are opened.

Fromage blanc et framboises
Fromage Blanc and Raspberries

Serves 2
Preparation: 5 minutes

4½ oz (125 g) fresh raspberries
9 oz (250 g) *fromage blanc* (fresh white cheese)
2 tsp granulated sugar (optional)

Equipment
3 ramekins with lids

1. Rinse the raspberries carefully with cold water, drain and place in a ramekin.
2. Divide the *fromage blanc* evenly between the two remaining ramekins. If desired, add a teaspoon of sugar to each serving. Accompany with the raspberries.

Chef's Tip
Raspberries can also be served "crushed": Put a few fresh raspberries in a small bowl, add two or three pinches of brown sugar and crush using a fork. The sugar will dissolve in the mixture, offsetting the acidity of raspberries.

Pain perdu et compotée d'abricots

French Toast and Apricot Compote

Makes 4 slices and 4 small bowls
Infuse: 1 hour
Preparation: 15 minutes + 30 minutes
Cook: 5 minutes + 25 minutes

Apricot Compote
18 oz (500 g) fresh apricots
¼ cup (50 g) superfine (caster) sugar
4 tsp (20 ml) lemon juice

French Toast
1¾ cups (400 ml) heavy (double) cream
½ vanilla bean (pod)
4 egg yolks
6½ tbsp (80 g) superfine (caster) sugar
4 slices round brioche (challah), 1 in (2 cm) thick
1 tbsp (15 g) unsalted butter

APRICOT COMPOTE

1. Wash, pit (stone), and cut the apricots into small pieces. Put the apricots into a saucepan, and sprinkle with the sugar. Cook over low heat, for about 25 minutes, stirring regularly until the fruit is tender. Then, stir in the lemon juice. Set aside.

FRENCH TOAST

2. Pour the cream into a saucepan. Cut the vanilla bean lengthwise into two pieces. Using the point of a knife, scrape the seeds into the cream; add the bean. Heat gently until the milk simmers. Remove from the heat and infuse for 1-hour. Then, discard the vanilla pod.

3. Combine the egg yolks and sugar in a bowl, beat until pale yellow and creamy. Stir in the infused cream, using a spatula.

4. Dip both sides of the sliced brioche into the egg mixture and lightly drain. Melt the butter gently in a large frying pan. Pan fry each side of the sliced brioche for about a minute, or until golden.

5. Accompany with the apricot compote. Serve immediately.

An Alternate Version

Why not make pistachio French toast? To do so, substitute the vanilla with a spoonful of pistachio paste, and whisk into the egg mixture. Or, perhaps you prefer cherry compote? Follow the recipe for the apricot compote using cherries instead of apricots.

The Art of Entertaining

Table Setting Etiquette

KNIFE HOLDERS, OR NOT?

The use of this table accessory is reserved for meals with family or close friends. It indicates that the host will not change the cutlery for every dish served.

Tableware

EXQUISITE UTENSILS AND ACCESSORIES

There are a variety of specific utensils and charming accessories including ivory, pearl or bone egg spoons; long-handled, almost flat ice-cream spoons; grapefruit spoons with one serrated side for cutting into and removing the segments; cake forks--usually with three short tines (prongs) one of which is flat and wider than the others; dessertspoons--larger than a teaspoon, and perfect for scooping up *crème anglaise* or *coulis*; cake servers and pastry tongs...even the tiny tool used to make butter curls (now somewhat out of fashion), just like the ones served in the past at Cabourg's Grand Hotel! Don't deprive yourself!

Setting the Stage

LIGHTING TO ENHANCE

In the morning, natural light is cold and quite harsh which is not always very flattering for the complexion...
Filter the luminosity using wispy curtains or blinds of thin linen, fine silk or organza... Add or correct the existing lighting with small lamps positioned in the room to create the mood. Avoid overhead, track or spot lighting because they are too bright and cast shadows on faces. And, why not light some pastel-coloured candles to add to the glow? All that is left now is to choose some soft, melodious background music...

FAMILY BREAKFAST

· ·●· ·

Baked Eggs with Cream

Fromage Blanc with Fresh Herbs

Fresh Fruit Salad

Citrus-Almond Bostocks

Chocolate Butter on Toast

· ·●· ·

Œufs cocotte à la crème
Baked Eggs with Cream

Serves 4
Preparation: 15 minutes
Cook: 6 minutes

4 tsp (20 g) softened butter
8 very fresh eggs
Salt, ground white pepper
1 cup (240 ml) *crème fraîche*
Fleur de sel (sea salt crystals)

Equipment
8 mini-cocottes with lids
8 ramekins
1 pastry brush

1. Brush the mini-cocottes with the softened butter; set aside.
2. Break the eggs into the ramekins; season with salt and pepper. Then, pour one seasoned egg into each buttered cocotte and cover with a lid. Line a roasting pan with baking parchment to stop the cocottes from lifting when the water in it boils. Put the cocottes into the pan; add hot water to come halfway up the sides of the cocottes.
3. Preheat the oven to 340°F, 170°C or gas mark 3. Bake the eggs for about 6 minutes until the whites are lightly set and the yolks still soft.
4. Warm the *crème fraîche*; season with salt and pepper. Remove the cocottes from the oven and cool slightly. Sprinkle the surface of the baked eggs with *fleur de sel* and nap with warm *crème fraîche*. Serve immediately.

Chef's Tip
Remember that the eggs will continue to cook when removed from the oven. Keep this in mind otherwise you will have hard-cooked eggs with cream!

Fromage blanc aux fines herbes
Fromage Blanc with Fresh Herbs

Serves 4
Preparation: 20 minutes

4 stalks chervil
4 stalks flat leaf parsley
4 stalks tarragon
8 chives
16 oz (480 g) *fromage blanc* (fresh white cheese)
Salt, ground white pepper
4 tsp (20 ml) extra virgin olive oil
Fleur de sel (sea salt crystals)

1. Set aside small sprigs of chervil, parsley, and tarragon for decoration. Remove the leaves from the herb stalks; discard the stalks. Finely slice (do not chop) the herb leaves and chives.
2. Season the *fromage blanc* to taste with salt and pepper; stir in the herbs.
3. Divide the *fromage blanc* evenly between four small tea cups, or verrines. Drizzle with the olive oil and sprinkle with *fleur de sel*. Decorate with the reserved herb sprigs.

Chef's Tip
If possible, use a mild fromage blanc, otherwise its flavour will dominate that of the herbs.

Make your own fromage blanc (fresh white cheese) to discover the real flavour. Following is an easy recipe for 4 servings: 4 cups (1 litre) of milk, liquid rennet, a bowl, and a clean white cotton dish (tea) towel and a strainer.

1. *Pour the milk into a saucepan and heat slowly to 95°F (35°C). Add 3 to 4 drops of liquid rennet to start curdling the milk. Pour the mixture into a bowl and cover with the dish towel. Set aside in a room with a minimum temperature of 68°F (20°C) for at least 12-hours until completely curdled.*
2. *Line the strainer with the dish towel to filter the curdled milk; strain. Then, transfer the contents of the dish towel (the fromage blanc) carefully into a separate bowl. Enjoy!*

To really appreciate the flavour of fresh fromage blanc, sweeten it with a little honey. Or, add fresh herbs as indicated in the recipe above. It can only be kept for 24 to 48-hours; refrigerate in an air-tight container.

...

Salade de fruits
Fresh Fruit Salad

Serves 4
Preparation: 25 minutes
Infuse: 2 hours

Spiced Syrup
4 cups (1 L) water
1¼ cups (250 g) granulated sugar
1 vanilla bean (pod)
Zest of 1 organic or untreated lime
1 star anise

Fresh Fruit Mixture
½ pineapple
½ mango
2 kiwis
5½ oz (150 g) strawberries
5½ oz (150 g) raspberries
3½ oz (100 g) blackberries
1¾ oz (50 g) blueberries

Spiced Syrup

1. Bring the water and sugar to the boil; stir until the sugar has completely dissolved. Add the vanilla, lime zest and star anise; remove from the heat. Set aside to cool and infuse for a minimum of 2 hours; strain.

Fresh Fruit Mixture

2. Use a sharp knife to remove the pineapple skin. Peel the mango and kiwis. Cut the fruit into bite-size pieces. Carefully rinse the strawberries, raspberries, blackberries and blueberries with cold water; drain. Hull and cut the strawberries in halves. Leave the other berries whole.

Assembly

3. Put all the fruit into a glass bowl and pour the cold (or chilled) syrup over it. Enjoy!

Bostocks aux agrumes
Citrus-Almond Bostocks

Makes 4 Bostocks
Preparation: 1 hour
Cook: 12 minutes

Citrus-Almond Cream
6 tbsp (90 g) unsalted butter, roughly chopped
¾ cup (100 g) confectioner's (icing) sugar
1 cup (100 g) ground almonds (almond flour)
2½ tsp (8 g) cornstarch (corn flour)
1 egg
2 tsp (20 g) candied lemon peel, finely chopped
1 tsp (10 g) candied orange peel, finely chopped

Citrus Syrup
1 organic or untreated lime
1 organic or untreated lemon
1¾ cups (450 ml) water
1 cup (200 g) granulated sugar
¼ cup (45 g) brown sugar

Assembly
4 slices round brioche (challah), 1 in (2 cm) thick
2 tbsp (25 g) sliced (flaked) almonds
Confectioner's sugar for decoration

Equipment
Piping bag fitted with a ⅜ in (10 mm) tip

Citrus-Almond Cream

1. Put the butter into a bowl over a *bain-marie* (water bath); soften until creamy but not melted. Remove the bowl from the *bain-marie*, add the confectioner's sugar, ground almonds, cornstarch, egg and candied citrus peels; stir well to combine. Fill the piping bag with the mixture; set aside.

Citrus Syrup

2. Zest the lime and lemon using a zester. Put the water, granulated and brown sugar into a saucepan. Bring to the boil, stirring until the sugar is completely dissolved. Remove from the heat and add the citrus zests.

Assembly

3. Set a cake rack on a baking sheet or tray. Line a baking sheet with baking parchment. Use a skimmer to quickly dip the brioche slices, one by one, into the hot syrup; drain on the cake rack. Put the drained slices on the baking sheet.
4. Preheat the oven to 340°F, 170°C or gas mark 3. Pipe a thin layer of citrus-almond cream on each brioche slice and scatter with sliced almonds. Bake for about 12 minutes, or until the edge of the citrus-almond cream is golden. Set the Bostocks aside to cool then, dust with confectioner's sugar. Consume the day prepared.

An Alternate Version

You could also prepare pecan-almond Bostocks. Replace the sugar in the syrup with chestnut honey. Make an almond cream exactly as indicated but without the candied citrus peels. And, finally, replace the sliced almonds with chopped pecans.

Beurre au chocolat et tartines grillées
Chocolate Butter on Toast

Makes 4 slices
Preparation: 15 minutes

7 oz (200 g) unsalted butter, roughly chopped
6½ tsp (50 g) unsweetened cocoa powder
3 oz (80 g) dark chocolate
4 thick slices country-style bread

1. Put the butter into a bowl over a *bain-marie* (water bath). Soften until creamy but do melt. Remove from the *bain-marie*, add the cocoa powder and stir well to combine.
2. Stand a block of chocolate on a piece of baking parchment. Hold it at a slight angle and use a small knife or a fixed-blade vegetable peeler to scrape off chocolate shavings.
3. Toast and cool the bread slightly before spreading with chocolate butter. Scatter with chocolate shavings. Enjoy!

An Alternate Version

Are you a milk chocolate lover? If so, substitute the cocoa powder with 2 oz (50 g) of melted milk chocolate and stir it into the softened butter. Leftover chocolate butter can be refrigerated for up to 1 week in an air-tight container.

The Art of Entertaining

Tableware

TEA SERVICES

A silver tea service... the teapot, a strainer and stand, sugar tongs, creamer, and a small hot water pot, decorated with garlands of rococo flowers and ribbons or engraved with Louis XVI-style beads...
In the 19th Century, serving tea was considered an art, especially when the consumption of tea became fashionable in high society circles. Silversmiths and porcelain manufacturers rivalled each other to create and offer exclusive tea services, as well as a myriad of delightful matching accessories. The English have also added a very practical but kitsch element...the tea-cosy. However, it should only be used with family.

Savoir-Faire

STEEP BUT NOT TOO MUCH

Tea is an infused beverage. However, unlike coffee, it needs a little time to steep. For each type of tea, there are ideal infusing times which are always indicated by the best tea merchants. Try to adhere to them when making tea otherwise it will have a tannic or even bitter taste. So, when entertaining you need to find a way of stopping the process. Here are some solutions: Put the tea leaves in a tea ball (large enough to let the flavours develop), or use a special paper filter. Either one can be removed from the teapot in the prescribed time. Or, prepare the tea in the kitchen and when brewed, pour it into the serving teapot (previously warmed... of course).

Expert Advice

A THERMOS OF HOT WATER

A thermos filled with hot water is ideal for diluting coffee or tea deemed too strong without getting up from the table.
It can even be used to prepare a sachet of herbal tea. Keep the thermos at hand, on a serving trolley or sideboard, but not on the main table.

Bijou Brunches

ELEGANT BRUNCH

· • ·

Pastrami Club Sandwich

Poached Eggs on Toast with Morel Mushrooms

Parisian Brioches Filled
with Creamy Green Vegetables

Kugelhopf with Pink Candied Almonds

Gingerbread

· • ·

Club sandwich au pastrami
Pastrami Club Sandwich

Makes 8 sandwiches
Preparation: 30 minutes
Cook: 2 hours

Oven-Dried Tomatoes
9 oz (250 g) tomatoes
1 tsp salt
4 tsp (20 ml) extra virgin olive oil

Lemon Sauce
1 tsp (6 g) salt
4 tsp (20 ml) lemon juice
4½ tbsp (70 ml) extra virgin olive oil

Filling
7 oz (200 g) celery root (celeriac)
6 tbsp (80 g) mayonnaise
12 oz (350 g) pastrami
3½ oz (100 g) cornichons (gherkins)
16 thin slices white bread, crusts removed
6½ oz (180 g) arugula (rocket)

OVEN-DRIED TOMATOES
1. Preheat the oven to 175°F, 80°C or gas mark less than ¼. Wash and slice the tomatoes ⅛ in (4 mm) thick, season with the salt and sprinkle with the olive oil. Put the slices onto a baking sheet and dry in the oven for 2 hours.

LEMON SAUCE
2. Put the salt and lemon juice into a bowl; whisk until the salt dissolves. Continue whisking and gradually add the olive oil. Set aside.

FILLING
3. Peel and grate the celery root; combine with the mayonnaise. Finely slice the pastrami; set four slices aside for decoration. Finely slice the cornichons. Toast the bread. Wash and finely slice the arugula; season with lemon sauce.

ASSEMBLY
4. Put a slice of toast on a cutting board, cover with some seasoned celery root and arugula, pastrami, oven-dried tomato and sliced cornichons; top with a piece of toast. Cut the sandwich in half. Repeat for the remaining seven sandwiches. Cut the reserved pastrami slices into 16 small pieces and attach decoratively to the sandwiches using toothpicks.

Chef's Tip
If desired, the club sandwiches could be accompanied with a green salad or French fries.

…

Œufs pochés aux morilles fraîches

Poached Eggs on Toast with Morel Mushrooms

Serves 8
Preparation: 15 minutes
Cook: 10 minutes

Morel Mushrooms
7 oz fresh (200 g) morel mushrooms
1 tbsp (15 g) butter
Salt

Poached Eggs
12 cups (3 L) water
3½ tbsp (50 ml) distilled white vinegar
2 tsp coarse salt
16 very fresh eggs

Assembly
4 slices white bread, crusts removed
Fleur de sel (sea salt crystals)
8 sprigs chervil

Morel Mushrooms

1. Rinse the morels gently in cold water. Repeat the operation twice being careful to remove all the impurities. Melt the butter in a medium frying pan. When it starts to foam, add the morels and season with salt; cook uncovered over low heat for 10 minutes.

Poached Eggs

2. Put the water, vinegar and coarse salt into a large, frying or sauté pan; bring to the boil. When the water comes to a rolling boil, reduce the heat until it simmers slowly and evenly.
3. Break an egg into a small ramekin. Position the ramekin just above the surface of the water. Slide the egg gently into the water. The white will wrap around the yolk and start to coagulate. Use two spoons to gather the white around the yolk to help enclose it. Or, push the egg carefully to the wall of the pan to seal the edges of the whites. Repeat for the remaining eggs.
4. Poach until the whites are firm to the touch but not rubbery, about 4 minutes. Use a skimmer to transfer the eggs to a bowl of cold water to stop the cooking and rinse off the vinegar.

Assembly

5. Toast the bread. Cut the toast slices diagonally into halves and place a poached egg on each half; sprinkle with *fleur de sel*. Decorate with the morels and chervil sprigs.

Brioches farcies aux légumes verts
Parisian Brioches Filled with Creamy Green Vegetables

Serves 8
Preparation: 35 minutes
Cook: 15 minutes

Creamy Green Vegetable Filling
3½ oz (100 g) green beans
3½ oz (100 g) snow peas
3½ oz (100 g) small green peas
3½ oz (100 g) fava beans
1 tbsp finely sliced tarragon leaves
Salt, ground white pepper
⅔ cup (150 g) plain yogurt

Assembly
8 Ladurée "Parisian" brioches
1 tbsp finely sliced parsley leaves
1 tbsp finely sliced chervil leaves
Extra virgin olive oil
Fleur de sel (sea salt crystals)

Creamy Green Vegetable Filling
1. Prepare a bowl of ice water. Cook the vegetables separately in boiling salted water (they should remain a little crunchy). Drain, refresh successively in the ice-water and drain again. Set aside. Cut the green beans and snow peas into slices ⅛ in (3 mm) wide and combine with the peas and fava beans. Add the tarragon; season to taste with salt and pepper. Drain the yogurt and stir into the seasoned vegetables.

Assembly
2. Cut the heads off the brioche bases using a serrated knife; set aside. Hollow out the centre of each base. Spoon the vegetable filling into the bases.
3. Put one filled base on each plate; re-place the heads. Decorate with parsley and chervil. Spoon a thin ribbon of olive oil around each brioche; sprinkle with *fleur de sel*.

Chef's Tip
Other vegetables, such as asparagus or flat green beans could also be used in this recipe.

Kouglof aux pralines roses
Kugelhopf with Pink Candied (Sugared) Almonds

Order this dessert from your local Ladurée patisserie.

Pain d'épices
Gingerbread

Serves 8
Preparation: 1 hour 30 minutes
Cook: 55 minutes
Infuse: 2 hours
Cool: 12 hours + 24 hours

⅔ cup (150 ml) water
5 star anise
5 tbsp (75 g) unsalted butter
½ cup (100 g) granulated sugar
⅓ cup (100 g) chestnut honey
Softened butter and flour for loaf pan
1 organic or untreated orange
1 organic or untreated lemon
1 scant cup (115 g) all purpose (plain) flour
1 cup + 1 tsp (110 g) rye flour
2 tsp baking powder
2 tsp ground cinnamon
1 tsp ground *quatre épices* (a blend of pepper, cloves, nutmeg, ginger)
2 tbsp (30 g) candied orange peel, diced

Equipment
Loaf pan 10 x 3 x 3 in (25 x 8 x 8 cm)
Grater

1. Combine the water, star anise, butter, sugar and honey in a saucepan; bring to the boil. Remove from the heat; infuse for 2 hours. Strain the liquid and cool overnight at room temperature.

2. Brush the loaf pan with softened butter. Cut a rectangle of baking parchment and line the bottom of the pan with it. Refrigerate for about 10 minutes until the butter hardens. Remove from the refrigerator, dust the pan with flour, turn upside-down and lightly tap out the excess. Zest the orange and lemon using a fine grater.

3. Combine the flours, baking powder, cinnamon and *quatre épices*; sift into a large bowl. Stir in the orange and lemon zests and the candied orange. Gradually add the cold infused liquid to the flour mixture, stirring with a wooden spoon until the batter is very smooth.

4. Preheat the oven to 410°F, 210°C or gas mark 6/7. Pour the batter into the prepared loaf pan, filling it to ¾ in (2 cm) below the rim. Bake for 10 minutes and remove from the oven. Use a small knife to make a lengthwise incision in the top crust of the gingerbread; immediately return it to the oven. Lower the temperature to 355°F, 180°C or gas mark 4. Continue baking for about 45 minutes, until a knife inserted into the centre of the gingerbread comes out clean.

5. Cool the gingerbread in the pan on a wire rack for 5 minutes. Turn it out onto the rack and cool for 24 hours, if possible.

The Art of Entertaining

Expert Advice
THE TABLE AND SEATING

Depending on the number of guests, the physical setting and equipment on hand, there are two options: A table large enough to accommodate everyone with all the dishes placed in the centre of it; or a buffet table with several small tables at which to seat your guests. If you have more than 15 people, the second option is preferable. Tables seating four to six guests are ideal. Keep in mind that a large variety of tables and chairs can be rented, as well as the appropriate table linens...

It's a Question of Style
DES FLEURS BELLES À CROQUER

Rose petals, tiny blue star-shaped borage flowers, orange-red nasturtiums, violets, primroses...there are all kinds of edible flowers, and some are even delicious! It is wise not to purchase them from a florist because those flowers have often been chemically treated. Edible flowers can sometimes be found in the fruit and vegetable section of supermarkets. Why not utilize the flowers from your garden (assuming you don't use pesticides)? Rose petals decorating a cake, or scattered over a dessert such as the *Fontainebleau*, can give that extra delightful touch of style... Consider using wildflower petals from dandelions, marigolds or poppies, to enhance a bowl of *fromage blanc*, a platter of fresh fruit, even ice-cream or sorbet. Decorate a citrus salad with violets for a stunning contrast.

Tableware
SOMETHING OLD... SOMETHING NEW!

Soup bowls, egg cups, small dishes and cups, salt cellars... Forget their original purpose and use them for serving compote, a cream, a few biscuits, spices or, some can even double as tiny vases to hold mini-bouquets of fresh mint...

ECCENTRIC BRUNCH

· • • • ·

"Surprise" Bread

Baked Goose Eggs with Tomato Compote

Salmon Marinated with Cardamom and Mint

Fruit Loaf Cake

Mango *Tatin* Tartlets

· • • • ·

Pain surprise
"Surprise" Bread

Serves 8
Preparation: 30 minutes
Cook: 7 minutes

---

8 cubes white bread, 3 ⅛ in (8 cm)
3 tbsp (45 g) melted butter
3½ oz (100 g) carrots
3½ oz (100 g) celery root (celeriac)
14 oz (400 g) crab meat
Juice of 1 lime
3 tbsp finely sliced chives
Salt, ground white pepper
½ cup (120 ml) *fromage blanc*

---

1. Preheat the oven to 355°F, 180°C or gas mark 4. Brush the bread cubes with the melted butter. Toast in the oven until golden brown, about 4 minutes. Set aside to cool.
2. Peel the carrots and celery root; finely dice ¹⁄₁₆ in (2 mm). Prepare a bowl of ice water. Cook the vegetables separately in boiling salted water (they should remain crunchy). Drain, refresh in the ice water, and drain again.
3. Season the crab meat with the lime juice, 2 tbsp of the chives and salt and pepper to taste.
4. Using a serrated knife, cut a ¾ in (2 cm) slice off the toasted bread cubes for use as hats. Carefully hollow-out the bases using a small spoon and without damaging the exterior crust. Put a thin layer of *fromage blanc* into each base, cover with some crunchy vegetables and a layer of crab; finish with the remaining vegetables and *fromage blanc*. Sprinkle with the rest of the chives, top with the hats and serve.

Chef's Tip
Cut the cubes out of a 3¼ lb (1.5 kg) loaf of white bread. Make bread-crumbs with the crusts and left-over pieces of bread. Or, use them to prepare a traditional bread pudding.

An Alternate Version
This recipe can be varied according to the seasons and your taste. Mayonnaise mixed with a soft-boiled egg would work well. In winter, replace the crab and vegetables with foie gras. In summer, why not combine the flavours of avocado and Alaska crab or lobster...?

HINT OF SPRING BRUNCH

·◦●◦·

Chicken, Cucumber
and *Fromage Frais* Finger Sandwiches

Smoked Salmon with Citrus Caviar

Truffle Omelette

Pearl Sugar Brioches

Rose Loaf Cake

·◦●◦·

Fingers au poulet, concombre et fromage frais

Chicken, Cucumber and Fromage Frais Finger Sandwiches

Serves 6
Preparation: 20 minutes

5½ oz (150 g) cooked chicken breast
½ small cucumber
2¼ oz (60g) *fromage frais* (fresh white farmer's cheese)
Salt, ground white pepper
12 thin slices white bread, crusts removed

1. Cut the cooked chicken breast into paper thin slices. Peel the cucumber, cut in half lengthwise and remove the seeds; finely slice. Season the *fromage frais* to taste with salt and pepper.
2. Spread the *fromage frais* over 6 bread slices, cover with the sliced chicken, cucumber and remaining bread. Cut the sandwiches into small rectangles. Serve immediately.

Chef's Tip
If the sandwiches are prepared in advance, wrap in wax (greaseproof) paper to keep them fresh and moist.

Saumon fumé au citron caviar

Smoked Salmon with Citrus Caviar

Serves 8
Preparation: 15 minutes

1 lb 12 oz (800 g) smoked Scottish salmon
5 Australian finger limes (citrus caviar)
16 slices white bread

1. Trim away and discard any remaining dark flesh on the smoked salmon; refrigerate.
2. Cut the finger limes lengthwise in halves and scoop out the pulp. The pulp is composed of very small crisp beads known as citrus caviar.
3. Toast the bread.
4. Mound the smoked salmon decoratively on the plates. Sprinkle with citrus caviar. Serve with the warm toast.

Chef's Tip

Finger limes (citrus caviar) are a native Australian citrus fruit. They resemble a finger and are about the same size, hence the name. When their small crisp beads burst in the mouth they have a tangy citrus taste offset by a note of pink grapefruit.

Omelette à la truffe
Truffle Omelette

Serves 8
Preparation: 20 minutes
Cook: 3 minutes

1 oz (25 g) Périgord truffles
16 very fresh eggs
⅓ cup (80 ml) heavy (double) cream
Salt, ground white pepper
1 tbsp butter
Fleur de sel (sea salt crystals)

1. Finely slice the black truffle and set aside. Some of the truffle will be used in the omelette, the remainder for decoration.
2. Break the eggs into a large bowl and whisk briskly. Add the cream, season to taste with salt and pepper; whisk again. Melt the butter in a large non-stick frying pan. Pour the egg mixture into the pan. Use a rubber spatula and constantly push the liquid from the outer edge of the omelette back into the centre to cook. Turn off the burner after 30 seconds. The centre of the omelette will be moist but will finish cooking from the residual heat; set aside to keep warm.
3. Spread the centre of the omelette with some of the sliced truffles. Roll the omelette up and cut it into large segments. Decorate with the remaining truffle and sprinkle with *fleur de sel*. Serve immediately.

Brioches au sucre
Pearl Sugar Brioches

Makes 12 mini or 6 small brioches
Preparation: 25 minutes + 30 minutes
Cook: 12-15 minutes
Rest: 5 hours + 2 hours 30 minutes

Brioche Dough
1¼ cups (140 g) cake flour
5 tsp (20 g) superfine (caster) sugar
½ scant tsp salt
⅕ oz (5 g) fresh baker's yeast
2 eggs
6 tbsp (90 g) unsalted butter, cut into small pieces

Assembly
Flour for the work surface
1 egg, beaten for glazing
7 tbsp (80 g) pearl (nib) sugar

Equipment
Pastry brush

Brioche Dough

1. Sift the cake flour into a bowl. Put the sugar and the salt on one side of the flour. Crumble the fresh yeast into small pieces and put it on the other side of the flour. Do not allow the yeast to come into contact with the sugar or the salt before starting to mix the dough because they will inhibit or stop its rising action.
2. Break the eggs into a bowl and whisk briskly. Pour about two-thirds of the beaten eggs over the flour, salt, sugar and yeast and start stirring with a wooden spoon; gradually add the remaining egg. Knead by hand until the dough starts to pull away from the sides of the bowl. Add the butter and continue kneading until all the ingredients are completely blended and the dough starts to pull away from the sides of the bowl again.
3. Put the dough into a clean bowl and cover with a damp dish (tea) towel or plastic wrap. Set aside at room temperature until the dough rises and doubles in volume, about 2½ hours. Punch down, or deflate the dough by folding it over on itself. Refrigerate for approximately 2½ hours; it will rise again while cooling.

Then, punch down or deflate as previously described. The dough is now ready for use.

Assembly

4. Line a baking sheet with baking parchment. Dust a work surface with flour. Put the dough on it and roll by hand into a log of even thickness. Divide the log into 6 equal portions for small brioches or 12 equal portions for mini-brioches. Flatten a portion of dough in the palm of the hand, fold the dough over on itself and form it into a tight ball. Place the ball on the baking sheet. Repeat for the remaining pieces of dough. Set aside at room temperature until doubled in volume, about 2½ hours. The warmer the temperature (do not exceed 86°F, 30° C), the faster the dough will rise.
5. Preheat the oven to 355°F, 180°C or gas mark 4. Brush the tops of the dough balls with the egg glaze and sprinkle with pearl sugar. Bake for 12 to 15 minutes until golden. Remove from the oven, cool slightly and serve warm.

Cake à la rose
Rose Loaf Cake

Makes 4 Portions
Preparation: 1 hour 30 minutes
Cook: 55 minutes
Rest: 12 hours

Cake Batter
Softened butter and flour for loaf pan
¾ cup + 2 tbsp (105 g) all purpose (plain) flour
1 tsp baking powder
2½ tbsp (35 g) unsalted butter
½ cup (125 g) superfine (caster) sugar
2 eggs
4 tbsp (60 ml) heavy (double) cream
1 pinch salt
1 tbsp (15 ml) rose syrup

Rose Syrup
5 tbsp (75) ml water
⅓ cup (60 g) superfine (caster) sugar
2 tsp (10 ml) rose water
2 tsp (10 ml) rose syrup

Equipment
Loaf pan 6 x 3 x 3 in (15 x 8 x 8 cm)

CAKE BATTER
1. Brush the loaf pan with softened butter. Cut a rectangle of baking parchment and line the bottom of the pan with it. Refrigerate about 10 minutes until the butter hardens. Remove from the refrigerator and dust with flour, invert and lightly tap out the excess.
2. Sift the flour and baking powder into a large bowl. Melt the butter in a small saucepan over low heat. Put the sugar into a bowl and whisk in the eggs, one by one. Whisking continuously, add the cream, salt and rose syrup. Use a spatula to fold in the flour and baking powder; add the warm melted butter.
3. Preheat the oven to 410°F, 210°C or gas mark 6/7. Pour the batter into the loaf pan. Bake 10 minutes, remove from the oven and make a lengthwise incision in the top crust of the loaf cake; immediately return it to the oven. Lower the temperature to 355°F, 180°C or gas mark 4. Continue baking for 45 minutes or until a knife inserted into the centre of the cake comes out clean.

ROSE SYRUP
4. Combine the water, sugar, rose water and rose syrup in a saucepan and stir over low heat until the sugar dissolves. Increa se the heat, bring to the boil and remove it from the heat immediately.

ASSEMBLY
5. Put a cake rack over a large plate. Turn the loaf cake out onto the rack. Reheat the syrup and ladle it generously over the loaf cake. Repeat this operation twice; if necessary, use the syrup that has collected in the plate. Set the rose loaf cake aside to cool for 12 hours before serving.

The Art of Entertaining

Setting the Stage

FLOWERS FOR THE MORNING

Don't forget to put a small bouquet of short-stemmed flowers on the table. Make sure they are very fresh, delicately perfumed and with dainty petals. Choose pastel or bright colours in harmony with the seasons to compliment the table setting and the mood of the moment such as: roses, lilac, sweet peas, forget-me-nots, lily of the valley, miniature Peruvian lilies, snowbells, Christmas roses or mock-orange flowers. Just before putting the vase on the table, spray lightly with water to give the impression of freshly picked, dew-covered flowers.

Tableware

TEA, COFFEE AND HOT CHOCOLATE CUPS

Cups as we know them, with a handle and a matching saucer, were not always as they are today. Prior to the 18th Century, drinks such as tea, coffee and chocolate were rare and when consumed, served in small bowls. In time, the French, German and English porcelain manufacturers decided to add a handle to the bowl, and not only gave it a saucer but a small cover too. This evolution led to the creation of different sizes of cups... Teacups became larger with deeper-round bowls, while coffee cups remained smaller. For quite some time, cups or bowls for hot chocolate, even had two handles...

Table Setting Etiquette

SMALL PLATES

Cheese and dessert are traditionally served on smaller plates, less than 8 in (20 cm). There is also a series of smaller plates, 4½ to 6 in (12 -15 cm). These are for salad or bread. The bread plate is always placed to the left of the main-course plate. Salad plates, often half-moon shaped, are placed to the right, but this type of plate is seldom used now. However, there exists a perfect way to make use of all these small plates...brunch!

Chic Picnics

PASTORAL PICNIC

· · ● · ·

Foie Gras and Truffle Terrine

Lobster Mini-Club Sandwiches

Vegetable Gaspacho

Strawberry-Rhubarb Cupcakes

Mint-Aniseed Macarons

· · ● · ·

…

Terrine de foie gras à la truffe

Foie Gras and Truffle Terrine

Serves 6
Preparation: 20 minutes
Cook: 20 minutes
Refrigerate: 1 hour + 2 days

1 whole fresh duck *foie gras*, 21 oz (600 g)
Salt, ground white pepper
2 tsp (10 ml) red Port wine
½ oz (10 g) black truffle
8 slices kugelhopf, or country-style bread

Equipment
Earthenware terrine with lid

1. Devein the *foie gras* using the tip of a small knife and place on a large flat-bottomed plate. Season evenly with salt and pepper; sprinkle with the Port. Cover with plastic wrap and refrigerate for about 1 hour.
2. Cut the truffle into paper thin slices.
3. Preheat the oven to 300°F, 150°C or gas mark 2. Place the large *foie gras* lobe in the bottom of the terrine and lay the truffle slices on it; cover with the small lobe and pack down tightly.

Put the terrine into a *bain-marie* (water bath). Cover and cook in the oven for 20 minutes.
4. Remove the terrine from the oven and cool. Lightly press the *foie gras* using the lid of the terrine and pour off the fat into a bowl*; strain. Seal the terrine tightly with plastic wrap, place a weight on the *foie gras* and refrigerate for 2 days before serving.
5. Toast the bread. Just before serving, remove the terrine from the refrigerator and carefully slice the *foie gras*. Serve with the kugelhopf or warm toast.

Chef's Tip

Use the following procedure if you wish to keep the foie gras for up to 10 days: Unmold the cooked foie gras and coat the interior of the terrine generously with the *strained foie gras fat (to stop oxidation). Return the foie gras to the terrine, seal tightly with plastic wrap, place a weight on top and store in the bottom of the refrigerator.
Remove the weight only after several days.
Accompany the foie gras with apples, figs, raisins or yellow and red fruit. Artichokes, leeks or beetroot, etc. could also be used.

Mini-clubs au homard
Lobster Mini-Club Sandwiches

Serves 6
Preparation: 30 minutes
Cook: 2 hours

9 oz (250 g) tomatoes
2 tsp (12 g) salt
4 tsp (20 ml) extra virgin olive oil
¾ head iceberg lettuce
5½ tbsp (80 g) mayonnaise
12 thin slices white bread, crusts removed
¾ oz (20 g) seaweed tartar
11 oz (300 g) lobster meat
4¼ oz (120 g) glasswort (samphire)

1. Preheat the oven to 175°F, 80°C or gas mark less than ¼. Wash and cut the tomatoes into 3/16 in (4 mm) slices. Place on a baking sheet and sprinkle with the salt and olive oil. Dry in the oven for 2 hours.
2. Finely slice the lettuce and season with the mayonnaise.
3. Toast the bread.
4. Put a slice of toast on a cutting board, cover with a little seasoned lettuce, some oven-dried tomato slices, a thin layer of seaweed tartar, a few pieces of lobster meat, and a little glasswort, followed by a few more tomato slices; place a second piece of toast on top. If necessary, trim the edges and cut into four mini-sandwiches. Repeat the process for the remaining sandwiches.

Chef's Tip
These sandwiches could be served with a green salad and French fries.

Gaspacho de légumes
Vegetable Gaspacho

Serves 6
Preparation: 35 minutes
Cook: 8 minutes
Rest: 12 hours

4 slices white bread
4 tbsp (60 ml) milk
3½ oz (100 g) shelled small green peas
7 oz (200 g) medium tomatoes
1 bell pepper (capsicum)
7 oz (200 g) cucumber
½ bunch (60 g) green onions (scallions)
4 stalks mint
2 stalks basil
1 clove garlic, peeled

1¼ tsp salt
¾ tsp ground Espelette pepper
2 tbsp (30 ml) extra virgin olive oil
¾ tsp ground white pepper
4 tsp (20 ml) Sherry vinegar

1. About 12 hours before starting, soak the bread in the milk.
2. The following day, cook the peas in boiling salted water, drain and set aside to cool.
3. Wash all the vegetables and herbs.
Peel and quarter the tomatoes. Quarter and seed the bell pepper. Peel and seed the cucumber. Peel and roughly chop the green onions. Remove the leaves from the mint and basil stalks; discard the stalks. If necessary, remove the garlic germ.
4. Put all the vegetables and herb leaves in a food processor and pulse for 1 minute. Squeeze the bread to remove the excess milk and put it into the food processor with the vegetable mixture. Add the salt, Espelette pepper, olive oil, white pepper and Sherry vinegar; process for 1 minute. Strain the gaspacho and, if necessary, adjust the seasoning; refrigerate before serving.

Cupcakes fraise et rhubarbe
Strawberry-Rhubarb Cupcakes

Makes 2 cupcakes
Preparation: 1 hour 30 minutes
Cook: 6 minutes + 30 minutes + 20 minutes

Rhubarb Compote
2 sheets (4 g) or
1½ tsp powdered gelatine
3½ oz (100 g) rhubarb
1½ tbsp (15 g) superfine (caster) sugar

Strawberry Juice
7 oz (200 g) strawberries
2 tbsp (25 g) superfine (caster) sugar

Strawberry Cupcakes
4 tsp (20 g) unsalted butter
Scant ½ cup (55 g) all purpose (plain) flour
½ tsp baking powder
6 tbsp (70 g) superfine (caster) sugar
1 egg
2 tbsp (30 g) heavy (double) cream
1 pinch salt
Few drops strawberry flavouring
Few drops red food colouring

Assembly
1¾ oz (50 g) pink marzipan

Equipment
Cupcake liners

Rhubarb Compote

1. Soften the sheet gelatine in a bowl of cold water. (If using powder soften in 1 tbsp (15 ml) cold water for 5 minutes.) Wash the rhubarb. Use a small knife to remove the stringy filaments. Cut the stalks into small pieces. Combine the rhubarb and sugar in a saucepan. Cook for 10 minutes, until softened. Squeeze the excess water from the sheet gelatine. Add the gelatine to the hot compote and stir until completely dissolved. Pour the rhubarb compote into a bowl and refrigerate.

Strawberry Juice

2. Carefully wash, hull and chop the strawberries. Place in a bowl and stir in the sugar. Cook in a *bain-marie* (water bath) over very low heat for 30 minutes. Cool, strain and set the juice aside.

Strawberry Cupcakes

3. Put the butter into a small saucepan over low heat. When melted, remove from the heat immediately. Sift the flour and baking powder into a small bowl. Put the sugar into a separate bowl and whisk in the egg. Continue whisking and add the cream and salt. Use a wooden spoon or rubber spatula to fold in the flour mixture and the warm melted butter. Stir in the flavouring and the food colouring.

4. Preheat the oven to 410°F, 210°C or gas mark 6/7. Spoon the batter into the cupcake liners, filling them to ¾ in (2 cm) below the rim. Bake for 20 minutes; remove from the oven. Insert the point of a knife into the centre of the cupcakes, if cooked it should come out clean and dry; set aside to cool.

Assembly

5. Use a small spoon to make an opening in the top of each cupcake. Pour a tablespoon of strawberry juice into each opening to moisten the cupcakes. Then, put a tablespoon of rhubarb compote into the openings. Roll out the pink marzipan. Cover the tops of the cupcakes with it.

Chef's Tip

If desired, decorate with whipped cream and/or fresh strawberries.

Macarons menthe-anis
Mint-Aniseed Macarons

Order this dessert from your local Ladurée patisserie.

The Art of Entertaining

Setting the Stage

A PICNIC BASKET FOR EVERYONE

If you only have a few guests, prepare elegant picnic baskets for everyone. Line the interior with white, or pastel linen tea towels, include a large monogrammed napkin (serviette), a few small flowery paper napkins or, if possible, plates with matching paper napkins, silver cutlery, coloured or crystal glasses (each basket could contain unmatched ones), a ribbon-festooned bread roll, a printed menu... Draw your inspiration from the aristocratic festivities organised within the grounds of English castles. Use tableware and accessories that conjure up an image of the countryside.

A Touch of Folly

BIRDS SINGING

To provide the musical atmosphere of your picnic...let birds take care of it! If you are holding the picnic in the garden, an aviary would be ideal; indoors, a simple bird cage containing some singing birds would suffice to delight your guests' ears but be careful, not all birdsong is melodious... The other option is CDs of birds singing to create the perfect illusion. A couple of chickens pecking the lawn would add a truly pastoral touch, if the garden is fenced.

Expert Tip

COOLNESS AND FRESHNESS GUARANTEED

If your guests find the temperature pleasant, it is probably a little too warm for the food. To keep it cool and looking good, use chilled flat freezer packs as placemats or trivets. Simply wrap in napkins or slide them under the cloth on the buffet table. Freezer packs can be purchased in electrical goods shops and supermarkets. Remember to put them in the freezer at least 12 hours prior to use.

COLOURFUL PICNIC

· · ● · ·

Lavender and Avocado *Éclairs*

Raw Vegetable Basket

Salmon Loaf

Lemon-Meringue Tart

Rose, Violet and Jasmine
White Chocolate *Tuiles*

· · ● · ·

Éclairs à la lavande et avocat

Lavender and Avocado Éclairs

Serves 6
Preparation: 40 minutes
Cook: 25 minutes

Choux Pastry
7 tbsp (100 ml) water
5 tbsp (75 g) unsalted butter
1 pinch salt
¾ cup (80 g) cake flour, sifted
3 eggs
Softened butter for baking sheet
1 egg beaten with 1 pinch salt for glazing

Lavender Glaze
1 sheet (2 g) or 1½ tsp powdered gelatine
7 tbsp (100 ml) heavy (double) cream
1 tbsp lavender flowers
1 pinch salt
Few drops purple food colouring

Avocado Filling
2 avocados
4 tbsp (60 ml) lemon juice
1½ tsp *fleur de sel* (sea salt crystals)
1 tsp ground white pepper
1 tbsp finely sliced sage leaves
2 oz (60 g) smoked swordfish, finely diced

Equipment
Piping bag fitted with a ⅜ in (10 mm) tip

Choux Pastry

1. Preheat the oven to 355°F, 180°C or gas mark 4. Put the water, butter and salt into a saucepan and bring to the boil; remove from the heat immediately. Tip all the sifted flour into the hot liquid. Beat vigorously with a wooden spoon until a thick, smooth dough forms. Return the saucepan to low heat and continue beating for 1 minute to dry the dough. Remove from the heat and place the dough in a bowl. Add the eggs one by one, beating well after each addition until the dough is smooth and shiny, and falls in a point from the spoon. Do not allow it to become too liquid.

2. Spoon the dough into the piping bag. Lightly brush a baking sheet with softened butter and pipe six 5 in (12 cm) fingers of dough onto it. Brush the tops with the egg glaze. Bake 25 minutes, or until dry and golden. Cool the choux puffs on a rack.

Lavender Glaze

3. Soften the sheet gelatine in a bowl of cold water. (If using powder soften in 1 tbsp (15 ml) cold water.) Bring the heavy cream and lavender flowers to the boil. Remove from the heat, cover and infuse for 5 minutes. Squeeze the excess water from the sheet gelatine. Strain the infused cream, add the salt and gelatine; stir until the

gelatine is completely dissolved. Add one or two drops of the food colouring to the lavender glaze to obtain the desired colour. Set aside.

Avocado Filling
4. Pit and peel the avocados. Crush the flesh with a fork, stir in the lemon juice, salt, pepper and sage; add the diced swordfish. Spoon the mixture into the piping bag.

Assembly
5. Use the piping tip to pierce the bases of the choux puffs in 2 places. Gently pipe the avocado filling into each one; dip the tops into the glaze. Enjoy!

Panier de crudités
Raw Vegetable Basket

Serves 6
Preparation: 30 minutes

Vegetables
2 medium cucumbers
18 oz (500 g) carrots
1 stick celery
1 cauliflower
1 broccoli
2 bunches radishes
18 oz (500 g) red and yellow cherry tomatoes
3½ oz (100 g) small tomatoes
1 head seasonal lettuce

Fromage Blanc *Sauce*
18 oz (500 g) *fromage blanc*
1 tbsp (15 ml) extra virgin olive oil
1 tbsp (15 ml) lemon juice
5 tbsp finely sliced fresh herb leaves
½ tsp salt

Tomato *Sauce*
1 chopped shallot
14 oz (400 g) *fromage blanc*
2 tbsp (30 ml) aged red wine vinegar
3 tbsp (50 g) ketchup
A few drops Tabasco®
6 chives, chopped
½ tsp salt

Vegetables
1. Peel and cut the cucumbers, carrots and celery into small sticks. Wash the cauliflower and broccoli, separate the florets from the heads and stalks and set aside. Clean the radishes. Wash the tomatoes and the lettuce. Wrap the vegetables separately in plastic (cling) wrap; refrigerate.

Fromage Blanc and Tomato Sauces
2. Put all the ingredients for the *fromage blanc* sauce into one bowl and the ingredients for the tomato sauce into another; stir well. Cover and refrigerate until required.

Assembly
3. Line a basket (or platter) with the lettuce, frilled-side out, and arrange the vegetables

decoratively in it. Spray lightly with water and cover with a damp dish (tea) towel until required.
4. When the guests arrive, remove the dish towel and serve the sauces on the side.

Chef's Tip
Salted whipped cream or taramasalata could be served with the vegetables. In speciality food stores, a variety of seasonings and sauces is available including: turmeric-carrot, spinach-mint, raspberry-balsamic and cherry-pepper.

Alternate Presentation
Purchase a piece of Styrofoam, cut it into the desired shape and cover with aluminium (tin) foil. Attach the vegetables with toothpicks. Keep them as close together as possible and arrange the colours harmoniously.

Cake au saumon
Salmon Loaf

Serves 6
Preparation: 25 minutes
Cook: 45 minutes

1¼ cups (150 g) all purpose (plain) flour
1 tsp baking powder
1 ⅔ cups (400 ml) 2% (semi-skimmed) milk
5 tsp (25 ml) sunflower oil
1¼ tsp salt
1 tsp ground white pepper
3 eggs
1¾ oz (50 g) fresh salmon
3½ oz (100 g) smoked salmon, finely sliced
1 tbsp finely sliced chives
3 tbsp (20 g) grated Comté (or gruyere) cheese

Equipment
Loaf pan 10 x 3 x 3 in (25 x 8 x 8 cm)

1. Preheat the oven to 355°F, 180°C or gas mark 4. Sift the flour and baking powder into a bowl. Gently whisk in the milk. Whisking continuously add 4 tsp (20 ml) of the sunflower oil; season with the salt and pepper. Add the eggs one by one. Whisk thoroughly after each addition to ensure the oil and eggs are well blended. Continue whisking until the batter is smooth.
2. Cut the salmon into ³/₈ in (10 mm) cubes. Add the cubed and smoked salmon, chives and grated cheese to the batter; stir well to combine.
3. Brush the loaf pan with the remaining teaspoon of oil. Pour the batter into the loaf pan. Bake for 45 minutes until the point of a knife inserted into the centre of the loaf comes out clean and dry. The salmon loaf can be eaten warm or cold, sliced or cubed.

Chef's Tip
Have fun letting your imagination run wild... Prepare this recipe using small individual moulds, round or even square cake tins.

Tarte au citron meringuée
Lemon Meringue Tart

Order this dessert from your local Ladurée patisserie.

Tuiles chocolat aux fleurs
Rose, Violet and Jasmine White Chocolate Tuiles

Makes 10 tuiles of each flavour
Preparation: 35 minutes

10½ oz (300 g) white chocolate, finely chopped
2 oz (60 g) chopped almonds, roasted
1 drop each red and violet food colourings
1 drop each rose, violet and jasmine flavourings

Equipment
Digital candy (confectionery) thermometer

---

1. Cut a large sheet of baking parchment into six strips 2½ x 8 in (6 x 20 cm).
2. Melt the chocolate slowly over a *bain-marie* (water bath); stir occasionally. Heat the chocolate until it reaches 113°F (45°C) maximum. Remove from the heat immediately, and cool, stirring until the temperature decreases to 79°F (26°C).

TEMPERED CHOCOLATE
3. Divide the chocolate evenly among 3 small bowls while the temperature is still 79°F (26°C). Slowly reheat the chocolate again over a *bain-marie* until the temperature reaches 82°F (28°C) maximum. (The chocolate has now been tempered.)

FLAVOURED CHOCOLATE
4. Divide the almonds evenly among the bowls. Add a drop each of red food colouring and rose flavouring to one bowl for the rose tuiles; a drop each of violet food colouring and flavouring to another bowl for the violet tuiles; and a drop of jasmine flavouring to the remaining bowl for the jasmine tuiles.

ASSEMBLY
5. Use a spoon to form 1½ in (4 cm) discs of chocolate on a baking parchment strip. Work quickly while the chocolate is still warm. Place the strip lengthwise over a rolling pin to form the tuiles into a slightly curved shape. When hardened, remove and carefully peel off the paper. Repeat for the remaining chocolate. Enjoy!

VIBRANT PICNIC

· · ● · ·

Devilled Goose Eggs

Vegetable Terrine, Fresh Tomato Sauce

Veal and Pork Pâté in a Pastry Crust

Pistachio-Sour Cherry Club Sandwiches

Rose and Coconut Meringues

· · ● · ·

Œufs d'oie mimosa
Devilled Goose Eggs

Serves 6
Preparation: 20 minutes
Cook: 12 minutes

---

3 goose eggs
1½ tsp salt
5½ tbsp (80 g) mayonnaise
3 oz (80 g) crab meat, shredded
4 tsp finely sliced parsley leaves
1 tsp ground white pepper

1. Put the goose eggs into a saucepan of water; add the salt. Bring to the boil, lower the heat, and cook for 12 minutes. Transfer to a bowl of iced water to cool.
2. Peel and cut the eggs lengthwise into halves. Remove the yolks and place in a bowl; crush with a fork. Combine half the crushed yolks with the mayonnaise. Stir in the crab meat and parsley, season with pepper. Spoon the crab mixture into the egg white halves and sprinkle with the remaining egg yolks.

Chef's Tip
If desired serve the devilled eggs on a bed of salad greens; accompany with toasted country-style bread. To prepare a homemade mayonnaise:

Put 1 room temperature egg yolk and 1 tsp mustard in a bowl; season with salt and pepper. Whisk until well combined. Whisking continuously, add ¼ cup of oil drop by drop until the mixture starts to thicken and emulsify. Continue whisking and add ½ cup oil in a thin, slow stream. Add a little lemon juice, if desired, just before serving.

Terrine de légumes sauce vierge
Vegetable Terrine, Fresh Tomato Sauce

Serves 6
Preparation: 1 hour
Cook: 1 hour 10 minutes + 25 minutes
Rest: 12 hours

Fresh Tomato Sauce
3½ oz (100 g) very ripe tomatoes
1¾ oz (50 g) shallots, finely sliced
10 basil leaves, finely sliced
1 lemon
3½ tbsp (50 ml) extra virgin olive oil
Salt, ground white pepper

Vegetable Terrine
14 oz (400 g) medium tomatoes
1½ tsp salt
5½ tbsp (80 ml) extra virgin olive oil
7 oz (200 g) eggplant (aubergines)
7 oz (200 g) zucchini (courgettes)
1½ tsp fresh thyme leaves
4¼ oz (120 g) onions, finely diced
3 oz (80 g) pitted black olives, chopped
10 basil leaves, finely sliced

Equipment
Loaf pan 8 x 3 x 3 in (20 x 8 x 8 cm)

Prepare the sauce and the vegetable terrine the day before serving.

FRESH TOMATO SAUCE

1. Fill a bowl with ice water. Bring a large saucepan of water to the boil. Make shallow cross-shaped incisions in the bases of the tomatoes and immerse in boiling water for 10 seconds. Transfer immediately to the ice water, peel, quarter and seed the tomatoes. Finely dice and place in a bowl; add the shallots and basil. Stir gently to combine.

2. Cut the lemon in half. Use a small knife to cut off all the skin (peel) and pith of one lemon half. Insert the knife on either side of the segments to cut out and release them without any membrane; discard the seeds. Finely dice the segments and add to the tomato mixture. Juice the remaining half lemon. Pour the juice and the 3½ tbsp (50 ml) olive oil over the tomato mixture; season to taste with salt and pepper. Set the sauce aside to marinate for 12 hours.

VEGETABLE TERRINE

3. Preheat the oven to 175°F, 80°C or gas mark less than ¼. Wash and slice the tomatoes ³⁄₁₆ in (4 mm) thick. Put the slices onto a baking sheet, season with salt and sprinkle with 4 tsp (20 ml) of the olive oil; dry in the oven for 1 hour. Set the oven-dried tomatoes aside.

4. Increase the oven temperature to 355°F, 180°C or gas mark 4. Cover a baking sheet with baking parchment. Wash the eggplant and zucchini and cut lengthwise into thin slices. Place the slices on the baking sheet; brush with 2 tbsp (30 ml) of the olive oil and sprinkle with the thyme. Bake for 10 minutes.

5. Put the remaining olive oil in a frying pan. Add the onions and cook slowly over low heat for 20 minutes. Add the olives and basil; continue cooking for 5 minutes.

6. Line the loaf pan with plastic (cling) wrap, leaving a long overhang around the edges. Put a layer of eggplant into the bottom of the pan, then a layer of the oven-dried tomatoes, followed by the onion mixture; cover with a layer of zucchini. Repeat until all the ingredients have been used, finishing with a layer of eggplant. Press down on the contents of the terrine and

fold the plastic wrap over the top. Cut a piece of cardboard the same size as the pan, lay it on the terrine and weigh it down (with tins of canned food); refrigerate for 12 hours.

7. Serve the terrine chilled; accompany with the fresh tomato sauce.

Chef's Tip

The vegetable terrine is a classic of the French culinary repertoire. It can be prepared year round, varying the vegetables according to the season.

Pâté en croûte
Pork and Veal Pâté in a Pastry Crust

Preparation: 1 hour
Cook: 1 hour 30 minutes
Rest: 24 hours

Pâté
10½ oz (300 g) pork (blade shoulder or loin)
7 oz (200 g) veal (shoulder or escalope)
1½ tsp salt
2 tsp ground white pepper
1 tsp (4 g) sugar
1 tsp ground nutmeg
2½ tbsp (40 ml) Cognac
2 oz (60 g) shallots, finely diced
2 oz (60 g) onion, finely diced
1 tbsp fresh thyme leaves
1 bay leaf
2 tsp chopped parsley
4 tsp (20 g) butter
2 eggs, beaten

Pastry
18 oz (500 g) all purpose (plain) flour
2½ tsp salt
1 tbsp (15 ml) oil
1 cup + 1 tbsp (250 ml) milk
9 oz (250 g) butter
1 egg beaten for glazing

Equipment
Loaf pan 10 x 3 x 3 in (25 x 8 x 8 cm)

PÂTÉ

1. Use a knife to chop half the pork and veal into small pieces. Finely grind the remainder in a food processor or meat grinder. Combine all the meat, salt, pepper, sugar and Cognac in a bowl; mix well. Put the shallots, onion, thyme, bay leaf and parsley on top of the meat mixture. Cover with plastic (cling) wrap and marinate in the refrigerator for 24 hours.

PASTRY

2. Sift the flour into a large bowl, make a well in the centre; put the salt and oil into it. Stir the oil and milk into the flour and mix until a relatively firm dough forms. Put the dough onto a work surface and flatten it with the palm of the hand. Cut the butter into strips and place a few on top of the dough; fold the dough over the butter to enclose it. Repeat this operation several times

until all the butter has been incorporated. Form the dough into a ball, tap a few times with a rolling pin to flatten it. Wrap the dough in plastic (cling) wrap and refrigerate for a minimum of 12 hours.

3. On the day of cooking, roll the dough out evenly into a long rectangle, about ¼ in (5 mm) thick. Fold it into thirds to form a square, give it 45° turn to the right and roll it out again. Repeat this operation twice, always turning the dough in the same direction.

ASSEMBLY

4. Finish the pâté: Remove the shallots, onions and herbs from the top of the meat, transfer to a frying pan and add the butter. Cook over low heat without colouring for a few seconds to remove the sharpness. Cool and add to the meat mixture. Add the eggs, and mix well to combine all the ingredients.

5. Preheat the oven to 425°F, 220°C or gas mark 7. Roll out the dough and put the pâté in the centre of it and brush with water. Enclose the pâté in the dough and place on a sheet of tin (aluminium) foil. Brush the dough with egg glaze and slide everything into the loaf pan.

6. Make 2 openings in the top of the dough. Roll-up two small cylinders of baking parchment and insert one in each of the openings. (These act as chimneys to let the steam escape during cooking.) Bake for 15 minutes.

Lower the oven temperature to 390°F, 200°C or gas mark 6 and continue baking for 1 hour 15 minutes. Slice when cold.

Chef's Tip

If desired, enclose a duck foie gras sausage in the centre pâté before baking. Serve the pâté with a salad of mixed young greens (mesclun). Season it with an olive and truffle oil vinaigrette and shavings of summer truffle.

Club sandwiches pistache-griotte
Pistachio-Sour Cherry Club Sandwiches

Order this dessert from your local Ladurée patisserie.

Meringues à la rose et meringues à la noix de coco
Rose and Coconut Meringues

Makes 100 miniature meringues of each flavour
Preparation: 40 minutes
Cook: 2 hours 30 minutes

Rose Meringues
1 cup (120 g) confectioner's (icing) sugar
4 egg whites
½ cup + 2 tbsp (120 g) superfine (caster) sugar
Few drops red food colouring
Few drops rose flavouring

Coconut Meringues
1 cup (120 g) confectioner's (icing) sugar
4 egg whites
½ cup + 2 tbsp (120 g) superfine (caster) sugar
Few drops coconut flavouring
½ cup (40 g) grated coconut

Equipment
Piping bag fitted with small fluted tip

ROSE MERINGUES
1. Preheat the oven to 210°F, 100°C or gas mark slightly less than a ¼. Cover a baking sheet with baking parchment. Sift the confectioner's sugar; set aside.
2. Put the egg whites into a clean, dry bowl and whisk until frothy. Add 3 tablespoons of the superfine sugar and whisk until firm. Add another 3 tablespoons of the sugar and whisk for 1 minute. Add the remaining sugar and continue whisking for another minute.
3. Add the red food colouring and rose flavouring.
4. Using a rubber spatula, gently fold in the sifted confectioner's sugar.
5. Spoon the meringue mixture into the piping bag. Pipe evenly spaced small, star shapes of rose meringue onto the prepared baking sheet. Bake for 2½ hours. Cook the meringues slowly. They should not colour too quickly and be dry when cooked. Store the cold meringues in an air-tight container.

COCONUT MERINGUES
6. Follow Steps 1 and 2 as noted above. Add the coconut flavouring. Fold in the sifted confectioner's sugar. Proceed as indicated in Step 5, dusting the piped meringues with the grated coconut before baking

The Art of Entertaining

Savoir-Faire

OUTDOORS...KEEP YOUR GUESTS COMFORTABLE

On bright sunny days, remember to have umbrellas available (they can be rented), and lots of straw hats in all shapes and sizes. Purchase a variety of ordinary hats and decorate them with long ribbons or flowers matching the colours of the event. Your guests could take them home as a souvenir... If the weather is cool, external heating and shawls would be a good idea. Also, think about placing insect repellent coils or candles around, to keep annoying insects such as mosquitoes and wasps at bay.

Expert Tip

IMPROVISED COOLERS

If the weather is very warm you will need to have a large quantity of ice cubes on hand. They can be ordered, or purchased at your local supermarket. Improvise containers such as old metal washtubs or very large flower pots... Decorate them with flowers, grape vines, ivy or even wisteria branches and fill with ice cubes to keep the bottles chilled.

Setting the Stage

NO GARDEN?
MAKE ONE INDOORS!

You don't have a garden but when springtime rolls around you have an irresistible urge for greenery?
Well then, bring the outside indoors! What about buying some turf? It can be purchased in rolls and placed almost anywhere (even on the dining room table... covered first with a protective oilcloth if the table is made of wood). What could be more original than bales of hay used as coffee tables? Cover them with coordinating tablecloths. Get out your most luxurious tableware and crystal. Decorate with bedding plants or petals. Suspend ivy from the light fixtures...

Family Lunches

LUNCH IN THE GARDEN

· • ·

Langoustine Carpaccio with Ginger

Beef Tenderloin,
Vitelotte Potato Purée and Chips,
Candied Violets

Orange Blossom *Religieuses*

· • ·

Carpaccio de langoustines au gingembre

Langoustine Carpaccio with Ginger

Serves 6
Preparation: 45 minutes
Freeze: 30 minutes

Langoustine Carpaccio
4 lbs (1.8 kg) raw langoustines (Dublin Bay prawns), or 5 – 6 medium langoustines per person

Seasoning
2 organic or untreated limes
¾ cup + 1 tbsp (200 ml) extra virgin olive oil
1½ tsp *fleur de sel* (sea salt crystals)
Ground white pepper
3 oz (80 g) ginger
3 oz (80 g) piece Parmesan cheese
3½ oz (100 g) arugula (rocket)

LANGOUSTINE CARPACCIO
1. Carefully shell the langoustines without damaging the flesh. Gently pull on the central vein running along the back to remove it. Lay the langoustines flat on a plate and freeze for 20 minutes until hardened.
2. Using a very sharp knife carefully cut the langoustines lengthwise into paper thin-slices. Arrange the slices decoratively on 6 plates and cover with plastic (cling) wrap; refrigerate.

SEASONING
3. Use a fine grater to zest one of the limes; set the zest aside. Juice the limes. Combine the lime juice and olive oil, season with salt and pepper and mix well; set the sauce aside.
4. Peel and finely dice the ginger. Stand the Parmesan on a piece of baking parchment; use a small knife or a vegetable peeler to make shavings. Rinse and dry the arugula.

ASSEMBLY
5. Decorate the plates of sliced langoustine with Parmesan shavings, ginger, lime zest and arugula. Just before serving, sprinkle with the lime juice sauce.

Chef's Tip
This fresh, tasty starter can be served not only at a simple summer lunch but also on festive occasions. Easy and quick to prepare, it could be an ideal solution for an improvised last-minute meal.

Filet de bœuf rôti à la purée de vitelottes et violettes cristallisées

Beef Tenderloin, Vitelotte Potato Purée and Chips, Candied Violets

Serves 6
Preparation: 1 hour
Cook: 44 to 48 minutes

Vitelotte Potato Purée
2 lbs 10 oz (1.2 kg) vitelotte (blue) potatoes
Salt
7 tbsp (100 ml) milk
5 tbsp (75 g) butter
Ground white pepper
Oil for frying

Beef Tenderloin Steaks
2 lbs 10 oz (1.2 kg) beef tenderloin (fillet of beef)
Salt, ground white pepper
4 tsp (20 g) butter

Assembly
Fleur de sel (sea salt crystals)
4¼ oz (120 g) candied (crystallized) violets

Vitelotte Potato Purée
1. Peel all the potatoes. Set 2 aside in cold water to make chips. Put the remaining potatoes in a saucepan, cover with cold water and add a little salt. Cook over low heat for 40 minutes until soft; drain. Heat the milk. Melt the butter. Mash the potatoes or use a food mill to obtain a purée. Stir in the hot milk, melted butter and season to taste with salt and pepper.
2. Drain, dry and finely slice the 2 reserved potatoes. Fill a large saucepan or deep fryer no more than one-third full with oil and heat to 355°F (180°F). Carefully lower the sliced potatoes into the hot oil and fry until golden; drain on absorbent paper. Immediately season the chips (crisps) with salt to retain the crunchiness.

Beef Tenderloin Steaks
3. Preheat the oven to 355°F, 180°C, or gas mark 4. Trim the beef and cut it into 6 steaks; season with salt and pepper. Put the 4 tsp (20 g) butter into a frying pan over high heat. Add the steaks and sear on both sides until browned. Transfer to the oven, cook for 4 to 8 minutes, or until done as desired.

Assembly
4. Set out 6 warm plates. Arrange 2 quenelles of vitelotte purée and a steak on each one. Sprinkle with *fleur de sel*, decorate with vitelotte chips and candied violets.

Chef's Tip

Make a "jus" with the beef trimmings: Heat a little oil in a pan, add the trimmings and brown. Chop an onion, a carrot and a stick of celery and add to the pan with a bouquet garni. Barely cover everything with water and cook for 30 minutes. Strain the cooking liquid into a saucepan and reduce to the desired consistency.

Religieuses à la fleur d'oranger

Orange Blossom Religieuses

Makes 4 religieuses
Preparation: 1 hour
Cook: 1 hour

Choux Pastry
1 cup + 1 tbsp (120 g) cake flour
6 tbsp + 2 tsp (100 ml) whole milk
6 tbsp + 2 tsp (100 ml) water
2½ tsp (10 g) superfine (caster) sugar
1 pinch salt
5½ tbsp (80 g) unsalted butter
4 eggs
Softened butter for the baking sheet

Orange Blossom Pastry Cream
1 ⅔ cups (400 ml) whole milk
4 egg yolks
6½ tbsp (80 g) superfine (caster) sugar
4 tbsp (30 g) cornstarch (cornflour)
5 tsp (25 g) unsalted butter
2½ tbsp (40 ml) orange blossom water

Orange Blossom Glaze
7 tbsp (105 ml) water
½ cup (100 g) superfine (caster) sugar
3 oz (80 g) white chocolate
7 oz (120 g) white fondant
1 tbsp (15 ml) orange blossom water

Assembly
4 silver dragées
Green food colouring

Equipment
Piping bag
5⁄16 in (8 mm) plain tip
3⁄16 in (4 mm) fluted tip

Choux Pastry

1. Preheat the oven to 345°F, 175°C or gas mark 3½. Sift the flour. Put the milk, water, sugar, salt and butter into a saucepan and bring to the boil; remove from the heat immediately. Tip all the sifted flour into the hot liquid. Beat vigorously with a wooden spoon until a thick, smooth dough forms. Return the saucepan to low heat and continue beating for 1 minute to dry the dough. Remove from the heat and place the dough in a bowl. Add the eggs one by one, beating well after each addition until the dough

is smooth and shiny and falls in a point from the spoon. Do not allow it to become too liquid.

2. Brush a baking sheet with softened butter. For the bases, spoon four mounds of dough, 2½ in (6 cm) in diameter, onto the baking sheet. For the tops, spoon four mounds of dough 1¼ in (3 cm) in diameter, onto the baking sheet. Bake 1 hour, or until well risen, dry and golden. Cool the choux puffs on a rack.

Orange Blossom Pastry Cream

3. Pour the milk into a saucepan and bring to the boil. Put the egg yolks and sugar into a bowl, beat until pale and creamy; add the cornstarch. Quickly whisk a third of the hot milk into the egg yolk mixture then, add the remaining milk. Return the mixture to the saucepan. Whisking continuously, simmer over low heat until it thickens. Boil for 1 minute while continuing to whisk. Pour the pastry cream into a bowl and when cooled, but not cold, stir in the butter. Cover with plastic (cling) wrap and set aside until cold.

4. Whisk the cold pastry cream until smooth and add the orange blossom water. Set a small quantity aside for decoration. Fit the piping bag with the plain tip and spoon the remaining pastry cream into it. Pierce a small hole in the flat side of each choux puff and fill with the pastry cream.

Orange Blossom Glaze

5. Combine the water and sugar in a saucepan. Bring to the boil and remove from the heat as soon as the sugar dissolves. Set the sugar syrup aside until cold. Melt the white chocolate in a bowl over a *bain-marie* (water bath). Warm the white fondant and 10 tbsp of sugar syrup in a saucepan. Stir in the melted white chocolate and orange blossom water.

Assembly

6. Dip the rounded side of the choux puff tops into the glaze and set aside. Dip the rounded side of the bases into the glaze. Put the small choux puffs on top of the bases. Place one dragée on top of each *religieuse* and set aside to firm. Stir a little green food colouring into the remaining pastry cream. Fit the piping bag with the fluted tip and spoon the pastry cream into it; pipe decoratively around the tops of the *religieuses*.

An Alternate Version

Make a rose petal religieuse: Prepare the pastry cream as indicated above and replace the orange blossom water with 1 tbsp (15 ml) rosewater, 3 tbsp (45 ml) rose syrup and 3 drops of rose oil. Prepare a rose glaze using: 3 oz (80 g) white chocolate, 7 oz (120 g) white fondant, 5 tbsp (75 ml) rose syrup, 4 drops rose oil and a few drops red food colouring. Follow the method for the orange blossom glaze.

The Art of Entertaining

Setting the Stage

THE CHARM OF PLACE CARDS

If you have more than six guests, set up your seating plan in advance and use place cards. Traditionally, guests' names are written on small folded cards. However, you may wish to do something a little more imaginative... Use old postcards and stick small labels on them indicating the guest's name. Attach coloured cards to the napkins (serviettes) with a ribbon. Write the names on flat pebbles, star fish, or a pine cone using a silver marker.

HAVE FUN WITH PAPER NAPKINS

A wide array of paper napkins is available in a multitude of colours and beautiful designs. They will give your table wonderful splashes of colour and could even evoke the theme of the meal. Choose the napkins carefully to coordinate with your dishes, tablecloths, and even the menu. Don't hesitate to use napkins of different sizes, designs and colours, rolled up or folded one inside the other and placed on the table, not for practical reasons, but simply to make the overall table setting prettier. Also, paper and classic cloth napkins could be used together.

Savoir-Faire

SEATING PLAN

Guest seating follows a definite protocol. If the hosts are a couple they are seated at either end of the table facing each other. Or, occasionally, they are seated in the middle, face-to-face on either side of the table. The guest of honour, or first-time guest, is seated to the right of the hostess and the guest's partner, to the left of the host. The second place of honour is to the left of the hostess and so on, until all the guests have been seated around the table.

Religieuses aux champignons sauvages

Wild Mushroom Religieuses

Serves 6
Preparation: 1 hour
Cook: 30 minutes
Rest: 2 hours

1¾ oz (50 g) morel mushrooms
10½ oz (300 g) white (button) mushrooms
1¾ oz (50 g) porcini (cep) mushrooms
¾ tsp powder or 1 sheet (2 g) gelatine
3 tbsp (45 ml) extra virgin olive oil
Salt, ground white pepper
¾ cup (200 ml) 2% (semi-skimmed) milk
1½ oz (40 g) shallots, finely diced
14 oz (400 g) *faisselle* (fresh white farmers) cheese
1½ tbsp finely sliced parsley leaves
6 small choux puffs, for the tops
6 large choux puffs, for the bases

Equipment
Piping bag fitted with a ⅜ in (10 mm) tip

1. Wash and dry the mushrooms. Cut two of the morels into three lengthwise pieces and set aside for decoration. Set a third of the white mushrooms aside for the glaze. Finely dice all the remaining mushrooms; set aside.

2. If using powdered gelatine soften in 1 tbsp (15 ml) cold water for 5 minutes. Soften the sheet gelatine in a bowl of cold water.

3. Heat 1 tbsp (15 ml) of the olive oil in a pan over low heat, add the reserved whole white mushrooms, season with salt and pepper and cook for 15 minutes. Add the milk and continue cooking for 5 minutes. Puree in a food processor until smooth; taste and adjust the seasoning. Squeeze the excess water from the sheet gelatine. Add the gelatine to the hot mushroom puree and process until completely dissolved. Set the choux puff glaze aside.

4. Heat 1 tbsp (15 ml) olive oil in a pan, add the shallots and cook without colouring until soft. Add the diced mushrooms and cook gently over low heat for 10 minutes; season with salt and pepper and set aside. Put the *faisselle* and sliced parsley into a bowl, add the cooked diced mushrooms; stir to combine. Taste and, if necessary, adjust the seasoning; spoon the filling into the piping bag.

5. Heat the remaining olive oil in a pan, add the reserved morel pieces and quickly brown. Use the piping tip to make a small opening in the choux puff bases. Pipe the filling into each one.

Dip the tops of the large choux puffs into the mushroom glaze and place each one on a plate. Then, repeat the operation for the small choux puffs. Place the small ones on top of the large. Decorate with the pieces of morel mushroom.

Chef's Tip

The choux puffs for this recipe can be ordered from your local bakery. The price of mushrooms is often excessive and can be off-putting; as a result, we pass up on the wonderful experience of cooking them. However, why not allow yourself that luxury from time to time? Choose the most beautiful and best looking mushrooms and make sure their surfaces are dry. At first glance, you will be able to spot the ones that have been around for too long.

Souris d'agneau à la vanille, pommes reinette

Lamb Shanks with Vanilla, Apple Compote

Serves 6
Preparation: 35 minutes
Cook: 6 hours

2 vanilla beans (pods)
6 lamb shanks
Salt, ground white pepper
7 tbsp (100 ml) extra virgin olive oil
1 lb 9 oz (700 g) pippin (russet) apples
3 tbsp (45 g) butter
Fleur de sel (sea salt crystals)

1. Preheat the oven to 175°F, 80°C or gas mark less than ¼. Cut the vanillas beans lengthwise into two pieces. Using the point of a knife, scrape the seeds from the bean into a bowl and set aside. Place the lamb shanks in a roasting pan. Pour the olive oil over the lamb shanks, season to taste with salt and pepper and place the pieces of vanilla bean on top. Cover the roasting pan tightly with several layers of tin (aluminium) foil. Roast for 6 hours until succulently tender.
2. Peel, core and cut the apples into ³⁄₈ in (10 mm) cubes. Melt the butter in a large pan over low heat. Add the apples and cook slowly for about 20 minutes. Season to taste with salt and pepper, stir in the vanilla seeds and continue cooking until soft. Set the compote aside to keep warm.
3. Remove the lamb shanks from the roasting pan, strain the cooking liquid into a pan; remove the fat. Place the pan over low heat and reduce the cooking liquid to the desired consistency.
4. Mound the apple compote on the plates and place a lamb shank on each one. Spoon a little sauce onto each serving and sprinkle with *fleur de sel*.

Chef's Tip
In French the words to describe a lamb shank are "souris d'agneau". The word souris came from the Latin, "musculus" implying a "small mouse" under the skin. Later it evolved into the word "muscle". "Agneau" is the French word for lamb.

Verrines Castiglione
Passion Fruit-Coconut Mousse Verrines

Makes: 6 verrines
Preparation: 1 hour 20 minutes
Cook: 2 hours
Refrigerate: 2 hours

Passion Fruit Jelly
2¼ tsp powdered or
3 sheets (6 g) gelatine
1⅔ cups (400 ml) passion fruit juice

Coconut Mousse
1½ tsp powdered or
2 sheets (4 g) gelatine
¾ cup (180 g) coconut puree
1 cup + 2 tbsp (125 g) coconut powder
7 tbsp (100 ml) heavy (double) cream

Coconut Meringue
½ cup (60 g) confectioner's (icing) sugar
⅓ cup (60 g) superfine (caster) sugar
2 egg whites
½ cup (60 g) confectioner's (icing) sugar
4¼ tbsp (30 g) coconut powder
1 slice fresh pineapple

Equipment
6 verrines
Piping bag fitted with a ¼ in (6 mm) fluted tip

Passion Fruit Jelly
1. Soften the powdered gelatine in 1 tbsp (15 ml) cold water for 5 minutes. Or, soften the sheet gelatine in a bowl of chilled water for 10 minutes. Heat ⅓ cup (80 ml) of the passion fruit juice in a small saucepan over low heat. Squeeze the excess water from the sheet gelatine. Stir the gelatine into the warm coconut puree until completely dissolved; stir the mixture into the cold passion fruit juice.
2. Divide the passion fruit juice mixture evenly among 6 verrines and refrigerate 20 minutes until jelled.

Coconut Mousse
3. Soften the powdered gelatine in 1 tbsp (15 ml) cold water for 5 minutes. Or, soften the sheet gelatine in a bowl of chilled water for 10 minutes. Heat ¼ cup (60 g) of the coconut puree in a small saucepan over low heat. Squeeze the excess water from the sheet gelatine. Stir the gelatine into the warm coconut puree until completely dissolved. Add the mixture to the remaining

puree and stir in the coconut powder. Whisk the cream until firm and clinging to the whisk then, carefully fold it into the coconut mixture.

4. Remove the verrines from the refrigerator. Pour the coconut mousse into the verrines on top of the jelly.

COCONUT MERINGUE

5. Preheat the oven to 210°F, 100°C or gas mark slightly less than a ¼. Cover a baking sheet with baking parchment. Sift the confectioner's sugar; set aside.

Put the egg whites into a clean, dry bowl and whisk until frothy. Add 5 tsp (20 g) of the superfine sugar and whisk until firm. Add another 5 tsp (20 g) of the sugar and whisk for 1 minute. Add the remaining sugar and continue whisking for another minute. Using a rubber spatula, gently fold in the sifted confectioner's sugar.

6. Spoon the meringue mixture into the piping bag. Pipe small, evenly spaced star shapes of meringue onto the prepared baking sheet.
Bake for 2 hours. Cook the meringues slowly. They must not colour too quickly and should be dry when cooked. Store the cold meringues in an air-tight container.

7. Just before serving, cut the pineapple into small sticks and place them on the coconut mousse. Decorate with coconut meringues. Enjoy!

Chef's Tip

Coconut tuiles would go well with the verrines. Here is the recipe: Combine the following in a bowl: 3 egg whites, ¾ cup + 1 tbsp (100 g) confectioner's (icing) sugar. Add 7 tbsp (100 g) melted butter and ¾ cup + 1 tbsp (100 g) flour. Then, add 5¾ tbsp (40 g) coconut powder. Refrigerate the "tuile" batter for 2 hours. Preheat the oven to 320°F, 160°C or gas mark 3. Cover a baking sheet with baking parchment. Spread small spoonfuls of batter in thin discs onto the baking sheet. Bake until golden. Use a palette knife to lay the tuiles over a rolling pin, while still warm and pliable, forming them into a slightly curved shape; store in an airtight container.

SPRING LUNCH

• • •

Garden Pea and Mint Gaspacho

Red Mullet, Carrots and Strawberries

Lemon Verbena Cream and Peach Tart

• • •

Gaspacho de petits pois et thé vert à la menthe

Garden Pea and Mint Gaspacho

Serves 6
Preparation: 30 minutes
Cook: 6 minutes
Refrigerate: 1 hour

6 stalks fresh mint
1 lb 2 oz (500 g) shelled small green peas
Salt
2 tsp (10 ml) mint syrup
¼ cup (20 g) Ladurée green tea leaves
½ cup + 2 tbsp (200 ml) heavy (double) cream
Ground white pepper
Extra virgin olive oil
Fleur de sel (sea salt crystals)

1. Bring a saucepan of water to the boil and immerse mint for 10 seconds; drain. Put the mint into a food processor; add a little cold water and process. Refrigerate the mint juice until cold.

2. Cook the peas in boiling salted water for 6 minutes; drain. Puree the peas in a food processor, until thick and very smooth. The puree will be bright green; season to taste with salt and add the mint syrup. Set aside in the refrigerator.

3. Heat the heavy cream until it starts to simmer; remove from the heat. Add the green tea leaves and infuse for 5 minutes. Strain the cream and refrigerate for 1 hour or until cold. Whisk the cream until thick and firm; season to taste with salt and pepper.

4. Divide the gaspacho evenly among 6 verrines or very small bowls. Place a quenelle of mint cream and a thin ribbon of olive oil on each serving; sprinkle with *fleur de sel*.

Chef's Tip

If desired, set a few mint and green tea leaves aside; use them to decorate the gaspacho. Green peas are spring vegetable. If fresh peas aren't available, do not hesitate to use frozen for this recipe. In winter, this soup could be served hot.

Rouget barbet carottes et fraises blanches

Red Mullet, Carrots and Strawberries

Serves 6
Preparation: 45 minutes
Cook: 20 minutes

Carrots
3½ oz (100 g) carrots
3½ oz (100 g) yellow carrots
3½ oz (100 g) purple carrots
3½ oz (100 g) white carrots
Salt, ground white pepper

Strawberries
2½ oz (70 g) red strawberries
7 tbsp (100 ml) aged red wine vinegar
2½ oz (70 g) white strawberries

Red Mullet
12 red mullet fillets, 3½ oz (100 g) each
Salt, ground white pepper
2 tbsp (30 ml) extra virgin olive oil

Assembly
4 tsp (20 g) butter
12 glasswort (samphire) shoots
6 tsp Ladurée strawberry jam
Fleur de sel (sea salt crystals)

Carrots
1. Peel and cut the carrots into lengthwise strips $^{1}/_{16}$ in (2 mm) thick. Prepare a bowl of iced water. Cook the different coloured carrots separately in boiling salted water for 2 to 3 minutes each. They should remain crunchy. Drain and transfer immediately to the iced water; drain again. Set aside on a large plate, between two dish (tea) towels.

Strawberries
2. Hull and puree the red strawberries in a food processor. Strain through a fine wire mesh strainer. Set the juice aside. Put the vinegar into a small saucepan over medium heat and reduce to half its original quantity. Add the strawberry juice, season with salt and pepper; set the strawberry-vinegar juice aside. Hull and quarter the white strawberries; set aside.

Red Mullet
3. Season both sides of the fish fillets with salt and pepper. Put the olive oil into a cold, non-stick frying pan. Place the fillets in it, skin side down and cook over low heat for 3 minutes. Turn the fillets carefully and cook for a further 2 minutes.

Assembly

4. Melt the butter in a pan over low heat, add the carrots and reheat.
5. Place a red mullet fillet on a plate, skin side down, cover with the multicoloured carrots and top with a mullet fillet, skin side up. Garnish with glasswort shoots and white strawberries. Spoon a little strawberry-vinegar juice onto the plate and a teaspoon of strawberry jam. Repeat for the remaining servings. Sprinkle with *fleur de sel*. Enjoy!

Chef's Tip

These mullets are small and a pinkish-red colour. The livers are often used in sauces and fillings. The flesh of the red mullet tends to be firm with a distinctive, delicate flavour. Pay close attention when cooking to avoid damaging the flesh. White strawberries are a new product and typically seasonal. If they are not available, use red ones.

Tarte pêche-verveine
Lemon Verbena Cream and Peach Tart

Serves 4
Preparation: 1 hour 5 minutes
Cook: 28 minutes
Rest: 12 hours
Refrigerate: 1 hour
Infuse: 15 minutes

Almond Sweet Pastry
½ cup + 1 tbsp (70 g) confectioner's (icing) sugar
6½ tbsp (100 g) unsalted butter, chilled
¼ cup (25 g) ground almonds (almond flour)
Pinch fleur de sel (sea salt crystals)
1 egg
1¾ cups (200 g) cake flour
Softened butter for the tart pan
Flour for work surface

Lemon Verbena Cream
2½ tbsp powdered or
5 sheets (10g) gelatine
1 ⅔ cup (400 ml) heavy (double) cream
1 cup (250 ml) milk
6 tbsp (75 g) superfine (caster) sugar
¼ cup fresh lemon verbena leaves
7 tbsp (100 ml) heavy (double) cream

Roasted Peaches
6 yellow peaches
2 tbsp (25 g) superfine (caster) sugar

Equipment
Tart pan, 8 in (20 cm) diameter
Dried beans

ALMOND SWEET PASTRY
1. Sift the confectioner's sugar. Cut the butter into small pieces and place in a bowl. Cream the butter using a wooden spoon, or place it in an upright mixer equipped with a flat beater. Blend in the following ingredients one by one: the confectioner's sugar, ground almonds, salt, egg and then, the flour. Mix until the ingredients just start to stick together. Roll the dough into a ball, flatten and wrap in plastic (cling) wrap; refrigerate for 12 hours. (If the dough is overworked, the cooked pastry will not be light and crumbly.)
2. Lightly butter the tart pan. Dust the work surface with the flour. Roll the dough out evenly to a thickness of $1/16$ in (2 mm) and line the tart pan with it. Refrigerate for 1 hour.
3. Preheat the oven to 340°F, 170°C or gas mark 3. Prick the dough with a fork so it will remain flat during cooking. Cut out a 12 in (30 cm) disc of baking parchment and carefully place it in the dough-lined pan, pressing the parchment into the angles. Fill with dried beans to hold the parchment in place during cooking.
4. Bake for 20 minutes until golden. Remove the tart shell from the oven and lift out the baking parchment and beans. If the pastry has not coloured sufficiently, return it to the oven to finish cooking. Remove from the oven and set aside until cold.

LEMON VERBENA CREAM
5. If using powdered gelatine, soften in 1 tbsp (15 ml) cold water for 5 minutes. Or, soften the sheet gelatine in a bowl of chilled water for 10 minutes. Put the $1 2/3$ cup (400 ml) double cream, milk and sugar into a saucepan and bring to the boil. Remove from the heat, add the verbena and infuse for 15 minutes. Squeeze the excess water from the sheet gelatine. Strain the infused cream, add the gelatine and stir until completely dissolved; set aside until cold.
6. Whisk the remaining cream until firm and clinging to the whisk. Fold it carefully into the cold verbena cream. Pour the mixture into the pastry shell and set it aside until firm.

ROASTED PEACHES
7. Preheat the oven to 320°F, 160°C or gas mark 3. Cover a baking sheet with baking parchment. Wash, pit and cut the peaches into eighths and place on the baking sheet. Sprinkle with the sugar. Roast in the oven for 8 minutes, remove and set aside until cold. Peel the peach sections and arrange decoratively on the tart. Enjoy!

The Art of Entertaining

Savoir-Faire

WHICH TABLECLOTH IS BEST?

Tables and tablecloths are usually round, square or oval. But there is nothing to say that a round cloth must be used on a round table. On the contrary, a square tablecloth on a round table will fall more elegantly. The same effect can be obtained using a rectangular cloth on an oval table. Put a padded or felt table protector under the cloth. It will not only make the fabric appear more luxurious but, at the same time, it will protect the table.

Expert Tip

THREE CLOTHS IN ONE

If you have a large number of guests for a meal but do not have a large enough tablecloth, use three medium-sized ones: Overlap two in the centre of the table; the ends falling towards the floor should be quite long. Place the third one on the top of the table, to cover the overlapping tablecloths.

A Matter of Style

A SMALL GIFT FOR EVERYONE

In France, a delightful American custom has been adopted: Guest favours...a small souvenir or gift for each guest.
It is the thought that counts, not the value of the object provided. A simple rose from the garden accompanied by a personal note written on a pretty card; an old family photo, printed and framed in a modern mini-frame (a wide range of frames is available in decorating stores); a small jar of home-made jam, labelled with each guest's name...

Afternoon Teas

A TOUCH OF ROSE

Rose Milkshakes

Minted Red Fruit Charlotte

Sour Cherry and Almond Ice Cream

Milkshakes à la rose
Rose Milkshakes

Makes 4 milkshakes
Preparation: 1 hour 30 minutes + 5 minutes
Freeze: 3 hours

Rose Ice Cream (1 qt/1 L)
2 cups (500 ml) milk
½ cup (120 ml) heavy (double) cream
4½ tbsp (70 ml) rose syrup
3½ tbsp (50 ml) rosewater
8 egg yolks
⅔ cup (130 g) superfine (caster) sugar

Milkshakes
2 cups (500 ml) whole milk, chilled
4 rose petals

Equipment
Ice cream/sorbet machine (maker)

ROSE ICE CREAM

1. Pour the milk and cream into a saucepan and bring to the boil. Remove from the heat and stir in the rose syrup and rosewater. Put the egg yolks and sugar into a bowl and beat until pale yellow and creamy. Continue whisking and pour a third of the hot milk-cream onto the egg yolk mixture. Whisk the mixture into the saucepan containing the remaining hot milk-cream.

2. Stirring constantly with a wooden spoon, cook over low heat until the mixture thickens. When it coats the back of a spoon, remove from the heat immediately (do not allow it to boil). Pour the rose cream into a large bowl. Stir continually for 5 minutes to cool.

3. At least 3 hours before serving, pour the rose cream into an ice cream machine and churn until soft and velvety. Spoon the ice cream into a container and freeze until required.

MILKSHAKES

4. Remove the ice cream from the freezer 10 minutes before using to soften it. Put 8 scoops of ice cream into the bowl of a food processor or blender, add the chilled milk and process until smooth. Divide the milkshake mixture evenly among 4 glasses. Serve immediately. Decorate with rose petals.

Chef's Tip

If necessary, prepare the ice cream several days in advance and freeze it. This recipe can be adapted to make a variety of flavours: coffee, chocolate, caramel... For fruit milkshakes, such as strawberry, simply combine 1¾ oz (50 g) strawberries, with milk and strawberry sorbet.

Charlotte menthe et fruits rouges
Minted Red Fruit Charlotte

Serves 4
Preparation: 2 hours 15 minutes
Cook: 10 minutes
Refrigerate: 2 hours 15 minutes

Sponge Batter
1 cup (120 g) all purpose (plain) flour
1 cup (120 g) potato starch (flour)
10 eggs
2¼ cups (250 g) superfine (caster) sugar
Few drops red food colouring

Minted Red Fruit Compote
½ tsp powdered gelatine or
1 sheet (2g) gelatine
7 oz (200 g) raspberries
7 oz (200 g) blackcurrants
5½ oz (150 g) sour cherries
¾ cup (150 g) superfine granulated (caster) sugar
½ tsp pectin powder
10 – 15 drops peppermint

Fromage Blanc Mousse
1½ tsp powdered gelatine or
3 sheets (6g) gelatine
1¼ cups (300 ml) heavy (double) cream, chilled
2 egg yolks
6½ tbsp (80 g) superfine (caster) sugar
2 tbsp (30 ml) water
9 oz (250 g) *fromage blanc*

Assembly
10 ½ oz (300 g) strawberries
3½ oz (100 g) raspberries
3 oz (80 g) blackberries
3 small sprigs mint

Equipment
8 in (20 cm) pastry ring, 2 in (5 cm) high
Pastry bag fitted with a ⅜ in (10 mm) tip

SPONGE BATTER
1. Combine and sift the flour with the potato starch; set aside. Separate the eggs. Put the whites into a clean, dry bowl and set aside. Put the yolks into a large bowl, add half the sugar and whisk until pale yellow and creamy. Use a clean whisk and whisk the egg whites until frothy ; gradually add the remaining sugar, whisking until smooth, shiny and stiff peaks form. Gently fold in the egg yolk mixture. Sprinkle the flour and potato starch over the mixture and gently fold it in: Put the spatula into the centre of the mixture, and bring it up the side of the bowl, lifting the mixture over the flour and potato starch to incorporate it, turning the bowl at the same time. Add a few drops of the red food colouring. The batter should retain its volume, be evenly blended and smooth.

2. Preheat the oven to 340°F, 170°C or gas mark 3. Cover three very flat baking sheets with baking parchment. Trace an 8 in (20 cm) circle on two of the baking sheets. Trace a rectangle 12½ x 4¾ in (32 x 12 cm) on the third one. Spread a ¼ in (5 mm) layer of sponge batter inside the rectangle using an offset palette knife. Spoon the remaining batter into the piping bag. Start piping in the centre of one of the traced circles, working outwards in a spiral to the edge. Repeat for the other circle. Transfer the baking sheets to the oven immediately and bake for 10 minutes. Set the sponge rectangle and discs aside until cold.

Minted Red Fruit Compote

3. If using powdered gelatine, soften in 1 tbsp (15 ml) cold water for 5 minutes. Or, soften the sheet gelatine in a bowl of chilled water. Put the raspberries, blackberries, sour cherries and half the sugar into a saucepan. Cook over low heat for 10 - 12 minutes until the fruit is tender. Combine the pectin with the remaining sugar and stir into the compote; boil for 1 minute. Squeeze the excess water from the sheet gelatine. Stir the gelatine into the compote until dissolved. Set aside until cold; add the peppermint to taste.

Fromage Blanc Mousse

4. Chill a bowl. If using powdered gelatine, soften in 1 tbsp (15 ml) cold water for 5 minutes. Or, soften the sheet gelatine in a bowl of chilled water. Pour the cream into the chilled bowl and whisk briskly until light and airy but firm; set aside. Put the egg yolks into the bowl of an electric mixer equipped with a whisk and beat on medium speed. Combine the sugar and water in a small saucepan, bring to the boil. Boil the sugar syrup for exactly 2 minutes. With the mixer running continuously, pour the hot syrup very slowly into the beaten yolks. Be careful as the syrup could splatter and burn your hands. (Also, for this step to be successful, the beater must be kept running.) Squeeze the excess water from the sheet gelatine. Add the gelatine to the egg yolk mixture. Continue beating until the mixture is completely cold. Put the *fromage blanc* into a bowl, and gently fold in the cold egg yolk mixture. Fold in the whipped cream using a rubber spatula.

Assembly

5. Turn the rectangle and discs of sponge over and carefully peel off the baking parchment. Cut the rectangle into two long bands, 2 in (5 cm) wide. Line the inside wall of the pastry ring with a sponge band. Continue with the second band and cut off the excess using a small knife. If necessary, trim the sponge discs to fit inside the lined pastry ring. Ideally, each one should be about ½ in (1 cm) thick. If not, use a sharp knife to trim the excess. Place one sponge disc inside the lined ring and spoon a ½ in (1 cm) layer of minted red fruit compote onto it; refrigerate for 15 minutes.

6. Rinse and pat dry the strawberries, raspberries, and blackberries. Hull and cut the strawberries lengthwise into strips ¼ in (5mm) thick. (Set half the fruit aside to decorate the charlotte.) Ladle a thin layer of *fromage blanc* mousse over the compote to come to the halfway mark on the pastry ring. Place the second sponge disc on top and scatter the remaining fruit over it. Cover with the *fromage blanc* mousse to come just below the rim of the pastry ring. Refrigerate for 2 hours, or until firm. Decorate the top of the charlotte with the remaining berries and sprigs of mint. Enjoy!

1. Carefully wash and pit the cherries. Puree the cherries to a food processor. Pour the puree into a saucepan, add the milk, cream and sugar; stir to combine.
2. Cook the mixture over low heat. Stir until the mixture simmers; do not allow it to boil. When it thickens and coats the back of a spoon, remove from the heat and pour into a bowl. Stir continually for 5 minutes to cool. Stir in the bitter almond extract.
3. At least 3 hours before serving, pour the cream mixture into an ice cream machine and churn until soft and velvety. Spoon the ice cream into a container and freeze until required.

Crème glacée griottes et amande
Sour Cherry and Almond Ice Cream

Makes 1 quart (litre)
Preparation: 30 minutes
Rest: 3 hours

1 lb (450 g) fresh sour (Montmorency) cherries
6 tbsp (90 ml) whole milk
6 cups (1.5 L) heavy (double) cream
¾ cup + 2 tbsp (180 g) superfine (caster) sugar
1 drop bitter almond extract

Equipment
Ice cream/sorbet machine (maker)

The Art of Entertaining

Setting the Stage

THINK PINK

Coordinate the colour of the decoration with that of the food to be served. First, if the theme of the menu is pink, think about the colour of the tablecloth and serviettes (dye them if necessary); put small vases of flowers on the table containing various pink hues, include roses of course, but also consider lisianthus, sweet peas and wallflowers... Fill small dishes with pastel-coloured confectionary such as macarons, bonbons and dragées. Then, find everything you have on the hand in these colours, such as scarves and shawls, and lay them on the couches, or end tables. And, for the event, replace your regular light bulbs with pink ones to give off a very soft light.

Savoir-Faire

INTRODUCTIONS AND CONVERSATIONS

It is the role of the hostess to put the guests at ease and set the tone. Do the people invited know each other? If not, when making the introductions, add one or two personal details (which you have thought about in advance) such as places of residence or holidays, hobbies or even professions... Look for things that your guests may have in common. This will help to get the conversation started.

Expert tip

RE-PLATE A PIECE OF SILVERWARE

Sometimes, in a second-hand shop, one is tempted by a beautiful teapot, a fish platter or pie server with worn silver plating. It is also possible that your inherited family silverware bears the marks of many years of loyal service. If so, consider re-plating to restore and bring them back to life. You will be delighted with the result. At the same time, the craftsman can remove any dents from your coffee pot or vegetable dish, or attach a broken handle... However, good re-plating is expensive and should perhaps only be considered for very worthwhile pieces.

DELICIOUS MORSELS

· · ● · ·

Viennese Coffee

Chocolate *Financiers*

Hazelnut-Cinnamon Shortbreads

Rose Chantilly Cream
& Vanilla Chantilly Cream

· · ● · ·

Café viennois
Viennese Coffee

Serves 6
Preparation: 15 minutes

Chantilly Cream
1¼ cups (300 ml) heavy (cream)
3½ tbsp (25 g) confectioner's (icing) sugar
1 pinch vanilla powder
(a few drops of vanilla extract)

Coffee
6 cups very hot coffee

Equipment
Piping bag fitted with a ½ in (13 mm) star tip

CHANTILLY CREAM
1. Put a round bottomed bowl in the freezer to chill. Refrigerate the cream until required (whisk only when very cold).
2. Pour the cold cream into the chilled bowl and whisk briskly. When it starts to thicken, add the sugar and vanilla; continue whisking until stiff peaks form. Spoon the Chantilly cream into the piping bag; refrigerate until required.

COFFEE
3. Prepare the coffee and pour it into the cups. Pipe a large rosette of Chantilly cream onto the coffee. Serve immediately.

Variation

Prepare a Viennese chocolate: Use the basic recipe for cold chocolate-orange cream (page 160), without the marmalade and orange zests...of course.
Then make a cinnamon Chantilly cream: Bring 2 cups (500 ml) heavy (double) cream to the boil, add ⅓ cup (40 g) confectioner's sugar and a cinnamon stick; refrigerate for 24 hours. Remove the cinnamon stick, whisk the cream and pipe large rosettes on the chocolate.

Financiers au chocolat
Chocolate Financiers

Makes approx. 20 Financiers
Preparation: 20 minutes
Cook: 6 to 8 minutes
Refrigerate: 12 hours minimum

5½ tbsp (80 g) unsalted butter
1 oz (25 g) dark (70%) chocolate
1¼ cups (150 g) confectioner's (icing) sugar
⅓ cup (40 g) all purpose (plain) flour
3 pinches baking powder
2 tbsp (15 g) unsweetened cocoa powder
½ cup (50 g) almond powder (flour)
4 egg whites
4 tsp butter, for the moulds

Equipment
Barquette (boat) moulds 3½ x 1½ in (9 x 4 cm)

1. Melt the unsalted butter in a saucepan over low heat. Melt the chocolate separately. Sift the confectioner's sugar, flour, baking and cocoa powders into a bowl, add the almond powder; stir to combine. Using a spatula, stir in the egg whites progressively, to avoid lumps. Stir in the lukewarm melted butter and chocolate.
2. Refrigerate the batter for a minimum of 12 hours.
3. Preheat the oven to 410°F, 210°C or gas mark 6½. Melt the butter. Use a small brush to butter the moulds; refrigerate until hardened. Fill to the three-quarter mark with the batter and place the filled moulds on a baking sheet.
4. Bake for 6 to 8 minutes. Remove the chocolate financiers from the oven and cool slightly. Unmold and place on a rack until completely cold.

Chef's Tip
The uncooked batter can be refrigerated for 2 to 3 days in a covered container. This way you can bake it as needed.

Sablés noisette et cannelle
Hazelnut- Cinnamon Shortbreads

Makes 25 – 30 shortbreads
Preparation: 35 minutes
Cook: 15 minutes
Refrigerate: 2 hours minimum

10 tbsp or 5½ oz (150 g) sweet (unsalted) butter
1 pinch *fleur de sel* (sea salt crystals)
¼ tsp ground cinnamon
⅓ cup (40 g) confectioner's (icing) sugar
1⅓ cups (120 g) hazelnut flour (powder)
1¾ oz (50 g) crushed hazelnuts
1 egg
1½ cups (170 g) cake flour
Flour for the work surface

Equipment
Round pastry cutter 2½ in (6 cm)

If possible, prepare the shortbread dough the day before baking. It will be much easier to roll out.

1. Cut the butter into small pieces and place in a bowl. Cream the butter using a wooden spoon. Add the remaining ingredients one by one, in the order listed above, mixing well after each addition.

(Or use an upright electric mixer equipped with a flat beater.) Mix until the ingredients just start to stick together, so that the shortbreads will be crisp and crunchy when baked.
2. Roll the dough into a ball and wrap in plastic (cling) wrap; refrigerate for a minimum of 2 hours.
3. Preheat the oven to 320°F, 160°C or gas mark 3. Cover a baking sheet with baking parchment. Dust the work surface with flour and roll out the shortbread dough to a thickness of $1/16$ in (2 mm). Cut out discs of dough using the cutter and place in staggered rows on the baking sheet. Bake for 15 minutes until golden. Cool on a rack.

Variation
To make almond and aniseed shortbread, use the same quantity of almonds as indicated for the hazelnuts; replace the cinnamon with $1/8$ tsp of aniseed.

Crème Chantilly à la rose et crème Chantilly à la vanille
Rose and Vanilla Chantilly Creams

Makes 2 cups (1/2 litre)
Preparation: 10 minutes

2 cups (500 ml) heavy (double) cream
⅓ cup (40 g) confectioner's sugar
2 tbsp (30 ml) rose syrup or
Seeds of ½ vanilla bean (pod)

1. Put a round bottomed bowl in the freezer to chill. Refrigerate the cream until required (whisk only when chilled).
2. Pour the cream into the chilled bowl. Add the rose syrup or the vanilla. Whisk briskly until light and airy but firm. Refrigerate until required.

The Art of Entertaining

Setting the Stage
CHOOSING THE FLOWERS

Flowers on a table contribute to its charm, provided they have been chosen carefully. Do not use flowers whose fragrance might compete with the aroma of the wine or the food being served. Avoid lilies, lily-of-the-valley, mock orange, gardenia etc.
They are wonderful in the garden or in an entry-hall but not on dining tables. Choose very fresh flowers that will last during the meal without dropping their petals on the table, such as roses in full bloom...

Savoir-Faire
WRITTEN INVITATIONS

If you plan to send written invitations, do not wait until the last minute. They should be sent out at least three weeks in advance. In doing so, you have every chance that your prospective guests will be able to accept. Also, if necessary, it will give you the opportunity to invite a couple of close friends to take the place of those unable to participate. Make sure that the invitation clearly indicates the date and time.
Also, be sure to include your full address and telephone number. A few details concerning the event, such as: "A Fireside Afternoon Tea" or, "A Picnic in the Garden", will give your guests an indication of the dress code.

Expert tip
HOT COFFEE

Unlike hot chocolate, it is impossible to reheat coffee (or tea) any other way than in a microwave. But, it can be prepared in advance in the kitchen. Keep the coffee warm in a thermos and, when you are ready, pour it into your best coffee pot... previously warmed, of course.

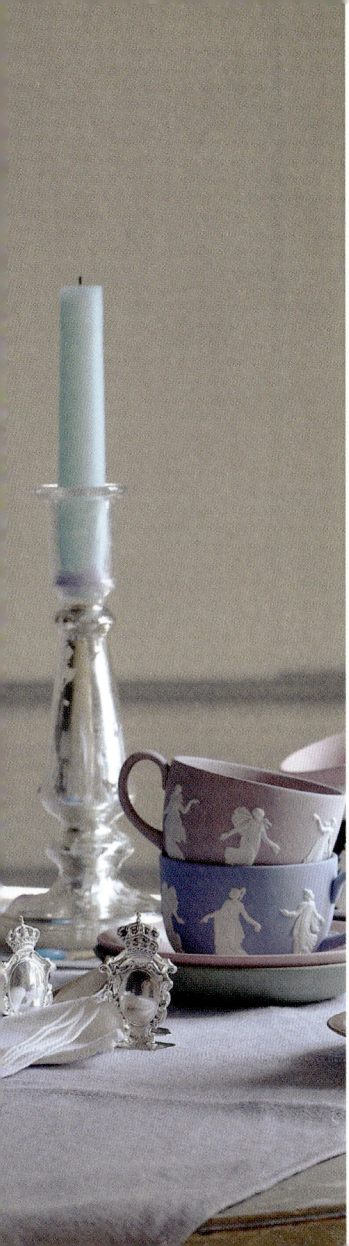

ESSENTIALLY CHOCOLATE

· ● ● ●·

Chocolate-Orange Cream

Chocolate-Raspberry Tartlets

Melon Sorbet

· ● ● ●·

Chocolat froid à l'orange
Chocolate-Orange Cream

Serves: 4 - 6
Preparation: 20 minutes
Refrigerate: 1 hour minimum

6½ oz (180 g) dark (70%) chocolate
1 organic or untreated orange
2½ cups (600 ml) whole milk
7 tbsp (100 ml) heavy (double) cream
1½ tbsp (35 g) orange marmalade

1. Coarsely chop the chocolate. Zest the orange using a vegetable peeler to remove strips of rind (without the pith). Cut the strips into matchsticks. Bring a small saucepan of water to the boil, blanch for 1 minute, drain and rinse under cold water. Set a few pieces of zest aside for decoration. Put the milk, cream and the remaining blanched zest into a saucepan; bring to the boil.
2. Remove the saucepan from the heat and whisk in the chocolate. Stir in the orange marmalade until the mixture is evenly combined and smooth.
3. Refrigerate the chocolate-orange cream until cold. Pour into glasses, decorate with the reserved orange zest and serve.

Variation
Replace the orange zests and marmalade in the chocolate cream either with 2 tsp (5 g) grated ginger, or 1½ tbsp (25 g) pistachio paste for every 4 cups (1 L) of hot or cold chocolate.

Tartelettes chocolat et framboise
Raspberry-Chocolate Tartlets

Makes 4 tartlets
Preparation: 1 hour 30 minutes
Cook: 20 minutes
Rest: Overnight
Refrigerate: 2 hours

Chocolate Pastry
8½ tbsp (130 g) unsalted butter
⅔ cup (80 g) confectioner's (icing) sugar, sifted
½ cup + 1 tbsp (70 g) ground almonds (almond flour)
2½ tbsp (20 g) unsweetened cocoa powder
1 egg
2 cups + 1 tbsp (250 g) all purpose (plain) flour, sifted
Unsalted butter for moulds
Flour for the work surface

Raspberry-Chocolate Ganache
11½ oz (320 g) dark (64%) chocolate, roughly chopped
7 tbsp (100 ml) heavy (double) cream
9 oz (250 g) fresh raspberries
5 tbsp (70 g) unsalted butter, chopped

Assembly
9 oz (250 g) fresh raspberries
3 oz (80 g) dark chocolate (optional)

Equipment
4 tartlet moulds, 3 in (8 cm) diameter
Dried beans
Digital candy (confectionery) thermometer

Chocolate Pastry

Prepare the dough the day prior to baking.
1. Cut the butter into small pieces and place in a bowl. Cream the butter using a wooden spoon. Blend in the following ingredients one by one: confectioner's sugar, ground almonds, cocoa powder, egg and then, the flour. Mix until the ingredients just start to stick together. Roll the dough into a ball and wrap in plastic (cling) wrap; rest in the refrigerator for 12 hours. (If the dough is overworked, the texture of the cooked pastry will not be crumbly.)
2. Butter the tartlet moulds. Dust the work surface with flour. Roll the dough out evenly to a thickness of $^1/_{16}$ in (2 mm) and line the moulds with it. Refrigerate for 1 hour.
3. Preheat the oven to 340°F, 170°C or gas mark 3. Prick the dough with a fork so it will remain flat during cooking. Cut out four 4 in (10 cm) discs of baking parchment. Put the parchment into the dough-lined moulds, gently pressing it into the angles. Fill with dried beans to hold the parchment in place during cooking.
4. Bake for about 20 minutes. Remove the tartlet shells from the oven and lift out the baking parchment and beans. If the pastry is not sufficiently cooked, return the tartlet shells (without the paper and beans) to the oven to finish cooking. Remove from the oven and set aside until cold.

Raspberry-Chocolate Ganache

5. Put the chopped chocolate into a bowl. Put the cream and the raspberries into a saucepan and bring to the boil. Use a stick blender to puree the mixture until smooth; strain using a fine-mesh wire strainer. Return the raspberry cream to the saucepan and bring to the boil. Pour the hot liquid over the chopped chocolate. Use a rubber spatula and stir gently in small circles from the centre to the outside of the mixture. Check the temperature and when it nears 122°F (50°C), stir in the butter.

Assembly

6. Ladle the raspberry-chocolate ganache into the tartlet shells using a small ladle; refrigerate for 1 hour, or until firm.
6. Remove the tartlets from the refrigerator and garnish with the fresh raspberries. If desired, decorate with chocolate shavings.

Variation

To make blackberry-chocolate tartlets, adapt the above recipe as follows:
10 oz (280 g) blackberries + 7 oz (200 g) for the garnish
1¼ cups (300 ml) heavy (double) cream
1 lb 2 oz (500 g) dark (64%) chocolate, finely chopped
7½ tbsp (110 g) unsalted butter, diced
1. Combine the blackberries and cream; puree using a stick blender. Strain to remove the seeds. Put the blackberry cream into a small saucepan; bring to the boil. Pour the hot liquid over the chocolate; stir gently using a rubber spatula. Add the butter and continue stirring until the mixture is thick and smooth.
2. Ladle the blackberry-chocolate ganache into the tartlet shells, refrigerate for a minimum of 1 hour, or until firm. Garnish with the remaining blackberries.

Sorbet au melon
Melon Sorbet

Makes approx. 1 quart (1 litre) sorbet
Preparation: 45 minutes
Rest: 3 hours minimum

½ cup (120 ml) water
1 cup + 2 tbsp (225 g) superfine (caster) sugar
21 oz (600 g) very ripe melon, finely diced
4 tsp (20 ml) lemon juice

Equipment
Ice cream/sorbet machine (maker)

1. Put the water and sugar into a saucepan, stir until the sugar dissolves and bring to the boil. Remove from the heat and set aside cool; refrigerate. Pour the cold syrup into the bowl of a food processor and add the melon. Process until smooth; add the lemon juice.
2. At least 3 hours before serving, pour the mixture into an ice cream machine and churn until soft and velvety. Spoon the sorbet into a container and freeze until required. (The sorbet can be kept frozen for several days.)
3. Remove the sorbet from the freezer 10 minutes before using to soften. Serve immediately.

Variation

If desired, infuse ½ a bunch of lemon verbena in the syrup. Strain the syrup before pouring it into the food processor. Or, make a vanilla-watermelon sorbet! Cut half a vanilla bean lengthwise in two pieces; infuse in the syrup. Replace the melon with exactly the same quantity of watermelon. Proceed as described.

The Art of Entertaining

A Question of Style

BEAUTIFUL UNMATCHED DISHES

When you mix-and-match sets of beautiful dishes, the effect produced is delightful. Ideally, it is best to choose a theme or a pattern such as the "*Royal Blue de Sevres*", white dishes with a coloured border, those with a hunting theme, the rose pattern from Limoges or Paris porcelain...
This will provide you with a variety of cups, ramekins and verrines, which will be much more appealing than serving everything on the same plate at your afternoon tea.
Use pretty vintage champagne saucers to serve fruit, a vanilla cream or chocolate mousse.

Savoir-Faire

SIT AT THE TABLE OR IN THE LIVING ROOM?

At an afternoon tea it is not necessary to sit around a table. The living (sitting) room would be an ideal place to welcome guests. However, ensure that the food being served can be easily consumed without using a knife... Provide a number of small side tables so that people can easily set down their cups, glasses or plates.

Expert tip

SERVE IT ON A TRAY

A tray is often the host's best friend! Plan to use several: one for sorbets or tartlets, another to serve the coffee or for the tea cups. Trays are also useful for removing used dishes. Prepare the trays in advance in the kitchen, so they will ready. Or, set them aside on a living room table.

Buffet Suppers

SUMMER EVENING BUFFET

· · ● · ·

Salty Ladurée Kisses

Vegetable Gratin, Jumbo Shrimp Brochettes

Regal Salad

Strawberries in Rosé Wine Soup

Lime-Basil *Éclairs*

Minted Strawberry Macarons

· · ● · ·

Baiser Ladurée salé
Salty Ladurée Kisses

Serves 6
Preparation: 20 minutes
Refrigerate: Overnight

2½ tsp powdered or
3½ sheets (7 g) gelatine
¼ cup (60 ml) heavy (double) cream
21 oz (600 g) fromage blanc
2½ oz (70 g) red currant tomatoes
1½ tbsp finely sliced basil leaves
1½ tbsp finely sliced chives
Salt, ground white pepper
6 small salted shortbread cookies (biscuits)
6 tsp (12 g) tapenade
Tomato powder
Fleur de sel (sea salt crystals)

Equipment
6 lip shaped moulds

---

1. Soften the gelatine powder in 2 tbsp cold water. Or, soften the sheet gelatine in a bowl of cold water.
2. Warm the cream in a small saucepan. Squeeze the excess water from the sheet gelatine. Add the gelatine to the warm cream; stir until completely dissolved. Add the *fromage blanc*, red currant tomatoes, basil and chives; season to taste with salt and pepper. Pour the mixture into the moulds and refrigerate for a minimum of 12 hours, or until firm.
3. Just before serving, spread each shortbread cookie with a teaspoon of tapenade then, turn out the lip shaped moulds. To highlight the shape of the lips, sprinkle with tomato powder. Dust lightly with *fleur de sel*. Enjoy!

Tian de légumes et brochettes de gambas
Vegetable Gratin, Jumbo Shrimp Brochettes

Serves 6
Preparation: 35 minutes
Cook: 30 minutes

Vegetable Gratin
2 medium eggplants (aubergines), finely sliced
1½ tsp (10 g) coarse salt
1 tbsp tarragon mustard
3 medium zucchini (courgettes), finely sliced
5 yellow tomatoes, finely sliced
5 roma (plum) tomatoes, finely sliced
5¼ oz (150 g) pineapple, finely sliced
3 tbsp (45 ml) extra virgin olive oil
Salt, ground white pepper

Jumbo Shrimp Brochettes
18 raw jumbo shrimp (king prawns)
1 tbsp (15 ml) extra virgin olive oil

Vinaigrette
1 tbsp tarragon mustard
4 tsp (20 ml) white balsamic vinegar
3 tbsp (45 ml) extra virgin olive oil

Assembly
1½ tsp wasabi sesame seeds
5¼ oz (150 g) Parmesan cheese shavings

Vegetable Gratin
1. Preheat the oven to 410°F, 210°C or gas mark 7. Sprinkle the eggplants with coarse salt to draw out the bitter juices and set aside for 20 minutes. Rinse and blanch the sliced eggplants in boiling water; drain.
2. Brush a gratin dish with the 1 tbsp tarragon mustard. Arrange all the sliced vegetables and pineapple overlapping in tight, alternating rows. Sprinkle with the olive oil and season to taste with salt and pepper. Bake for 20 minutes.

Jumbo Shrimp Brochettes
3. Season the shrimp with salt and pepper. Set out 6 skewers and put 3 shrimp on each one. Put the olive oil in a pan over medium heat and cook the shrimp on each side for 2 minutes. Set aside to keep warm.

Vinaigrette
4. Put the tarragon mustard in a bowl, season to taste with salt and pepper. Whisk in the white balsamic vinegar and, whisking continuously, slowly add the olive oil.

Assembly
5. As soon as the gratin comes out of the oven, arrange a rosette of vegetables on each plate. Top with the skewers of jumbo shrimp and sprinkle with wasabi sesame seeds. Decorate with Parmesan cheese shavings.

Chef's Tip
This recipe is a traditional gratin from Provence. It is economical, simple to prepare and full of flavour. As well, thanks to the vegetables, it is full of vitamins. If you do not like eggplant, or zucchini, make the gratin with the vegetable you prefer. For the 'meat-lovers', lightly pan fry a little bacon or sausage meat and put it in the gratin with the vegetables.

Salade royale
Regal Salad

Serves 6
Preparation: 20 minutes
Cook: 2 hours

14 oz (400 g) medium tomatoes
8 tsp (40 ml) extra virgin olive oil
3 tsp salt
4 small purple artichokes
1 lemon
2 large raw artichoke hearts
11 oz (300 g) arugula (rocket)

3½ tbsp (50 ml) balsamic vinegar
Salt, ground white pepper
7 tbsp (100 ml) walnut oil
14 oz (400 g) air-dried beef (bresaola), finely sliced
¼ cup (50 g) grilled corn kernels
3½ oz Parmesan cheese shavings
12 small sprigs chervil
Fleur de sel (sea salt crystals)

1. Preheat the oven to 175°F, 80°C or gas mark less than ¼. Wash and thinly slice the tomatoes. Put the slices onto a baking sheet, drizzle with 4 tsp (20 ml) of the olive oil; season with the 1½ tsp of salt. Dry the sliced tomato in the oven for 1 hour.
2. Snap the stems off the purple artichokes; cut off and discard the outer leaves. Cut each one lengthwise into 6 slices. Season with the remaining salt and olive oil and dry in the oven for 1 hour. Prepare a large bowl of cold water. Cut the lemon in half, squeeze a few drops of lemon juice into the water; add the lemon halves. Finely slice the large artichoke hearts. Put slices into the bowl of cold lemon water to avoid oxidation; set aside. Wash the arugula and set aside wrapped in a dish (tea) towel.
3. Prepare the vinaigrette: Put the balsamic vinegar into a bowl, season with salt and pepper to taste and whisk to dissolve the salt; whisk in the walnut oil.
4. Drain the raw artichoke heart slices and combine with a little vinaigrette; set aside. Put the arugula, oven-dried tomato and purple artichoke slices into a large bowl; season with the remaining vinaigrette.
5. Place a mound of salad on each plate. Top with the air-dried beef slices. Scatter corn kernels over the salads. Decorate with Parmesan shavings, the seasoned raw artichoke slices and chervil sprigs. Sprinkle with *fleur de sel*.

Chef's Tip
This salad is easy to prepare and full of flavour. It would be ideal at a lunch, or on a simpler buffet where each of the main ingredients could be seasoned and served separately, allowing guests to compose their own salads. Also, as arugula has a strong taste, most people prefer to eat it mixed with other salad leaves.

Soupe de fraises au vin rosé
Strawberries in Rosé Wine Soup

Serves 4
Preparation: 30 minutes
Cook: 5 minutes
Refrigerate: 2 hours

1 bottle (750 ml) *Côtes de Provence* rosé wine
¾ cup (150 g) superfine (caster) sugar
1 vanilla bean (pod)

1 cinnamon stick
18 oz (500 g) fresh strawberries
2 tbsp mint leaves
4 star anise

1. Put the wine, sugar, vanilla and cinnamon into a saucepan and bring to the boil. Remove from the heat and set aside to infuse for 30 minutes; strain and reserve the cinnamon stick. Refrigerate the "soup" for about 2 hours until chilled.
2. Wash and hull the strawberries. Cut the strawberries lengthwise into 4 or 6 slices, depending on the size. Divide the slices evenly among 4 small bowls. Finely slice the mint leaves and cut the cinnamon stick in 4 pieces.
3. Ladle the chilled rosé wine soup over the strawberries. Scatter with sliced mint leaves. Decorate with the pieces of cinnamon stick and the star anise.

Variation
If serving children with this recipe, make a grenadine and vanilla syrup. The ratio is 1 part grenadine syrup to 7 parts water. Infuse an unheated quart (1 L) of this preparation with a vanilla bean; chill and pour over sliced strawberries as indicated above.

Éclairs citron vert et basilic
Lime-Basil Éclairs

Makes 4 Eclairs
Preparation: 20 minutes
Cook: 1 hour
Refrigerate: 12 hours

Choux Pastry
7 tbsp (100 ml) whole milk
7 tbsp (100 ml) water
2 tsp (10 g) superfine (caster) sugar
1 pinch salt
3½ tbsp (80 g) unsalted butter
1 cup + 1 tbsp (120 g) cake flour, sifted
4 eggs
Softened butter for baking sheet

Lime and Basil Cream
1 organic or untreated lime
¾ cup + 1 tbsp (170 g) superfine (caster) sugar
1½ tsp (5 g) cornstarch (cornflour)
3 eggs
½ scant cup (115 g) lime juice
1 tbsp finely chopped basil
9 oz (250 g) unsalted butter, softened

Basil Glaze
7 tbsp (100 ml) water
½ cup (100 g) superfine (caster) sugar
3 oz (80 g) white chocolate

4¼ oz (120 g) white fondant
4 fresh basil leaves, finely sliced

Equipment
Piping bag fitted with a ⅝ in (16 mm) plain tip
Piping bag fitted with a ⅜ in (8 mm) plain tip

Choux Pastry

1. Preheat the oven to 345°F, 175°C or gas mark 3½. Put the milk, water, sugar, salt and butter into a saucepan and bring to the boil; remove from the heat. Tip all of the flour into the hot liquid. Beat vigorously with a wooden spoon until a thick, smooth dough forms. Return the saucepan to low heat and continue beating for 1 minute to dry the dough; remove from the heat and transfer the dough to a bowl.
2. Add the eggs one by one, beating thoroughly after each addition until the dough is smooth and shiny and falls in a point from the spoon. Do not allow it to become too liquid.
3. Spoon the dough into the piping bag fitted with the ⅝ in (16 mm) tip. Lightly brush a baking sheet with softened butter and pipe four 6 in (15 cm) fingers of dough on it. Bake 1 hour, or until dry and golden. Cool the choux puffs on a rack.

Lime and Basil Cream

4. Zest the lime using a fine grater. Put the zest into a bowl. Stir in the sugar, then the cornstarch; add the eggs one by one. Add the lime juice and basil. Pour the mixture into a saucepan and cook over low heat, stirring continuously with a spatula, until it simmers and thickens; remove from the heat.
5. Cool the lime basil cream for about 10 minutes until the temperature is 140°F (60°C). Add the softened butter and beat until thick and creamy. Refrigerate in an airtight container for 12 hours, or until firm.

Basil Glaze

6. Put the water and sugar into a saucepan over medium heat. Stir until the sugar dissolves and bring to the boil; remove from the heat immediately. Set the syrup aside until cold. Melt the white chocolate in a bowl placed over a *bain-marie* (water bath). Warm the fondant and ⅔ cup (150 ml) of the cold syrup in a saucepan over low heat. Add the melted white chocolate and basil; stir gently until smooth.

Assembly

6. Use the ⅜ in (8 mm) tip to pierce 3 holes in the bottom of each choux puff: make one in the centre and two others, about ¾ in (20 mm) from each end. Spoon the lime and basil cream into the piping bag equipped with the ⅜ in (8 mm) tip. Gently pipe the cream into each choux puff then, dip the tops into the basil glaze. Set aside until the glaze firms before serving the lime-basil *éclairs*.

Macarons fraise mentholée
Minted Strawberry Macarons

Order this dessert from your local Ladurée patisserie.

The Art of Entertaining

Savoir-Faire

A CHAIR FOR EVERY GUEST

Whatever the number, make sure that you have one chair available for every guest. If necessary, chairs can be easily rented. Put small side tables in various locations around the rooms to be used. If you live in a house with a garden and you have invited a large number of guests, consider renting a marquee, preferably with a floor. This will avoid damage to your lawn...and the guests' high heels.

Setting the Stage

WHITE WITH GOLDEN AND PASTEL HIGHLIGHTS

Cover and protect easily damaged sofas and chairs with large white sheets. This will also completely change the decor! Simply add some gilded decorating objects, such as a vase, a frame or small gilt spoons...
Include a few pastel touches such as a cushion, a tablecloth, plates... The object is to radiate comfort, beauty and calm!

Tableware

A WATER GOBLET

Usually, water is served in large stemmed glasses. However, why not serve it in silver goblets (like the ones given for births or baptisms...) or mugs? The water glass does not necessarily have to match the other tableware being used, and will provide a certain touch of originality. For example, choose red Bohemian crystal, or a more modern style such as simple yellow or turquoise water glasses to create an interesting effect. Water glasses are placed to the left of wine glasses.

AUTUMN SUNSET BUFFET

· · ● · ·

Vegetable Ravioli, Kaffir Lime Cream

Cheese Soufflé

Smoked Organic Salmon and Salsola Salad

Mushroom Tart

Veal *Piccata*, Lemony Orzo Risotto

Saint-Honoré Gâteau

Orange-Passion Fruit Macarons

Linzertorte

· · ● · ·

Ravioles de légumes au citron kaffir

Vegetable Ravioli, Kaffir Lime Cream

Serves 6
Preparation: 25 minutes
Cook: 15 minutes

Vegetable Ravioli
4 cups (1 L) water
2 tsp coarse salt
5¼ oz (150 g) green beans, finely diced
3½ oz (100 g) carrots, finely diced
3½ oz (100 g) zucchini (courgettes), finely diced
3½ oz (100 g) small green peas
1 small organic or untreated lime
Salt, ground white pepper
48 ravioli dough sheets (wonton wrappers)

Kaffir Lime Cream
¾ cup + 1 tbsp (200 ml) heavy (double) cream
2 tsp finely sliced kaffir lime leaves
4 tsp (20 g) butter

Assembly
1 medium carrot, thinly sliced
Chervil sprigs
Fleur de sel (sea salt crystals)

Equipment
Round pastry cutter 2½ in (6 cm)

Vegetable Ravioli

1. Prepare a large bowl of iced water. Pour the water into a saucepan, add the salt and bring to the boil. Blanch the green beans, carrots, zucchini and peas for 2 minutes. The vegetables must remain crunchy. Set ¼ cup (60 ml) of the blanching liquid aside. Drain the vegetables, refresh in the iced water to stop the cooking; drain again.

2. Use a fine grater to zest the lime. Combine the zest and the vegetables, mix gently and season to taste with salt and pepper.

3. Cut the ravioli sheets into discs using the pastry cutter. Spread half the discs out on a work surface. Put a spoonful of the vegetable mixture in the centre of each one. Lightly brush the exposed dough with water and cover with the remaining sheets; press down well on the edges to seal. Put the ravioli onto a plate, cover with plastic (cling) wrap and refrigerate.

Kaffir Lime Cream

4. Put the heavy cream and sliced kaffir lime leaves into a saucepan. Simmer for 10 minutes then, strain. Add the reserved blanching liquid and stir in the 4 tsp (20 g) butter. Set aside to keep warm.

Assembly

5. Cut the carrot lengthwise into thin slices; cut each slice into 3 pieces. Cook for 2 minutes in boiling salted water; drain. Bring a large quantity of salted water to the boil. Cook the ravioli for 2 to 3 minutes; drain. Serve immediately in soup plates. Nap with the kaffir lime cream. Decorate with carrot and chervil sprigs. Dust with *fleur de sel*.

Soufflé au fromage
Cheese Soufflé

Pour 6 personnes
Préparation : 50 mn
Cuisson : 20 mn

4½ tbsp (50 g) butter
⅓ cup + 1½ tbsp (50 g) all purpose (plain) flour
2 cups (1/2 L) whole milk
1 pinch ground nutmeg
6 egg yolks
Salt, ground white pepper
5¼ oz (150 g) Comté cheese, grated
10 egg whites
Softened butter for the soufflé moulds
Flour for the soufflé moulds
1 oz (25 g) Comte cheese shavings
Fleur de sel (sea salt crystals)

Equipment
6 individual soufflé moulds or 6 large ramekins

1. Melt the butter in a saucepan and whisk in all the flour at once to make a roux. Cook the roux for 2 to 3 minutes whisking continuously without colouring; remove from the heat until cold. Pour the milk into a separate saucepan, add the nutmeg and bring to the boil. Whisk the milk briskly into the cold roux and cook, whisking continuously over medium heat for 4 to 5 minutes.

2. Remove the mixture from the heat and whisk in the egg yolks one by one. Season to taste with salt and pepper and cook for another 2 to 3 minutes. Pour the mixture into a bowl, stir in the grated cheese and set aside to cool.

3. Preheat the oven to 390°F, 200°C or gas mark 6½. Brush the moulds with softened butter and dust with flour.

4. Put the egg whites into a bowl; add a pinch of salt. Whisk until the egg whites are smooth, shiny and stiff peaks form. Whisk a third of the beaten egg whites into the cheese mixture; gently fold in the remainder. Fill the moulds to the ¾ mark with the mixture. Bake for about 20 minutes until puffed and golden. Decorate with Comté cheese shavings. Dust with *fleur de sel*. Serve the soufflés immediately.

Chef's Tip

A soufflé must not be kept waiting, when it starts to cool it will fall.

Salade Salsola au saumon fumé bio

Smoked Organic Salmon and Salsola Salad

Serves 6
Preparation: 20 minutes

---

9 oz (250 g) salsola (sea mustard)
12 walnut halves
½ tsp (4 g) salt
2 tbsp (30 ml) balsamic vinegar
¾ tsp (2 g) pepper
4 tbsp (60 ml) walnut oil
1 lb 4 oz (550 g) organic salmon fume, sliced

---

1. Wash the Salsola and set aside in a damp dish (tea) towel.
2. Preheat the oven to 320°F, 160°C or gas mark 3. Put the walnut halves on a baking sheet and roast in the oven for 7 minutes. Set aside to cool.
3. Put the salt in a bowl, add the balsamic vinegar and whisk until the salt dissolves. Add the pepper and progressively whisk in the walnut oil.
4. Put the salsola into a salad bowl. Arrange the smoked salmon on a pretty serving platter and scatter the walnut halves over it. Serve the vinaigrette on the side.

Chef's Tip

Salsola is of Japanese origin. It is also known as the seaweed that grows on land, and sometimes called sea mustard. Salsola is crunchy and juicy with a spicy, salty taste and is rich in vitamin A, calcium and potassium. If you are unable to find it, use lettuce and add some samphire (sea asparagus) to obtain a give you a similar flavour.

•••

Tarte fine aux champignons

Mushroom Tartlets

Serves 6
Preparation: 30 minutes
Cook: 25 minutes

---

4 ½ oz (120 g) medium white (button) mushrooms
1 oz (30 g) yellow oyster mushrooms
1 oz (30 g) king oyster (eryngy) mushrooms
¾ tsp whole grain mustard
½ tsp strong Dijon mustard
6 discs puff pastry dough, 6 in (15 cm) diameter
6 tsp (30 ml) extra virgin olive oil
Salt, ground white pepper
⅓ cup (20 g) mustard seed sprouts

1. Rinse and dry all the mushrooms carefully. Cut the white (button) mushrooms into 3/16 in (4 mm) slices. Tear the yellow oyster mushrooms into strips. Cut the king oyster mushrooms lengthwise into two pieces. Finely slice the heads. Finely dice the stems. Set all the mushrooms aside.
2. Preheat the oven to 380°F, 195°C or gas mark 5½. Put the whole-grain and Dijon mustards into a bowl; stir to combine. Cover a baking sheet with baking parchment and place the puff pastry discs on it. Coat the discs of puff pastry dough with the mixed mustards using a pastry brush. Arrange a rosette of white mushrooms on each disc and place the yellow and king oyster mushrooms on top. Sprinkle with the olive oil and season to taste with salt and pepper.
3. Transfer to the oven and bake for 10 minutes. Lower the heat to 320°F, 160°C or gas mark 3 and continue baking for 15 minutes.
4. Scatter the mustard seed sprouts over the tartlets just before serving.

Chef's Tip

In France, the king oyster mushroom is known as "eryngii" or "pleurote du panicautit"; the botanical name is pleurotus eryngii *; it has the reputation of being one of the most flavourful cultivated mushrooms. The stem can be very thick and bulging, similar to the porcini mushroom. Depending on the season, use other varieties of mushrooms including: morels, porcinis, chanterelles, or even truffles.*

«Piccata» de veau, citron confit et risotto d'avoines
Veal Piccata, Lemony Orzo Risotto

Serves 6
Preparation: 20 minutes
Cook: 20 minutes

1 lb 12 oz (800 g) milk fed veal rump (chump end)
Salt, ground white pepper
5 tbsp (75 ml) extra virgin olive oil
3½ tbsp (50 g) butter
4 cups (1 L) chicken stock
2 small shallots, finely chopped
7 oz (200 g) orzo (risoni) pasta
3½ tbsp (50 ml) white wine
2 oz (60 g) Parmesan cheese, finely grated
2½ oz (70 g) mascarpone
4 tbsp (20 g) preserved lemon jam
1 oz (25 g) Parmesan cheese shavings
Fleur de sel (sea salt crystals)

1. Trim and cut the veal into 6 equal portions.
2. Preheat the oven to 355°F, 180 F or gas mark 4. Season the veal with salt and ground white pepper. Put a sauté pan over high heat, add 2 tbsp (30 ml) of the olive oil and sear the veal portions evenly. Put the veal into an

ovenproof dish, dot with the butter and finish cooking in the oven for 8 minutes.

3. Heat the chicken stock and keep it warm. Put the remaining 3 tbsp (45 ml) of olive oil into a large pan over medium heat. Add the shallots and cook without colouring for 2 minutes. Add the orzo pasta and cook for 2 minutes until translucent but not coloured. Add the white wine and stir continuously until evaporated.

4. Add the chicken stock ladle by ladle, giving the pasta sufficient time to absorb the liquid in between each addition; stir regularly. Cooking time will be about 20 minutes. Taste from time to time to check the texture of the pasta; it should be cooked but remain 'al dente'.

5. Stir in the grated Parmesan, mascarpone and preserved lemon jam. Taste and adjust the seasonings.

6. Serve the orzo risotto in soup plates, decorate with Parmesan shavings and sprinkle with *fleur de sel*. Cut the veal portions into thin strips; serve on the side.

Chef's Tip

Veal piccata is a dish of Italian origin where the meat is cut into strips prior to cooking.
In this recipe, to keep the meat juicy, it is cooked gently and evenly in larger portions and sliced after cooking. This risotto is a variation on a theme. Instead of the traditional Arborio rice, orzo (risoni) pasta has been used.

Saint-honoré au caramel
Saint-Honoré Gâteau

Order this dessert from your local Ladurée patisserie.

Macarons orange-passion
Orange-Passion Fruit Macarons

Order this dessert from your local Ladurée patisserie.

Tarte « linzer » à la framboise
Linzertorte

Serves 6
Preparation: 1 hour
Cook: 33 minutes
Refrigerate: 13 hours

Cinnamon Pastry
1 cup (120 g) confectioner's (icing) sugar
2¼ cups (250 g) cake flour
10 tbsp (150 g) unsalted butter, chilled
7½ tbsp (75 g) almond flour (powder)
2 tsp cinnamon
2 eggs
Softened butter for the tart pan
Flour for the work surface

Raspberry Preserves
1 lb 12 oz (800 g) fresh raspberries
1¼ cups + 2 tbsp (280 g) superfine (caster) sugar

Equipment
1 round, 8½ in (22 cm) tart pan

Cinnamon Pastry

1. Sift the confectioner's sugar and flour separately. Cut the butter into small pieces and place in a bowl. Cream the butter using a wooden spoon, or in an upright mixer equipped with a flat beater. Blend in the following ingredients one by one: the confectioner's sugar, almond flour, cinnamon, eggs and then, the flour. Mix until the ingredients just start to stick together. Roll the dough into a ball and wrap in plastic (cling) wrap; refrigerate for 12 hours. (If the dough is overworked, the texture of the cooked pastry will not be crisp and crunchy.)

2. Butter the tart pan. Dust the work surface with flour. Roll the dough out evenly to a thickness of ¹⁄₁₆ in (2 mm) and line the tart pan with it. Refrigerate for 1 hour. Cut the remaining dough into strips the same length as the diameter of the tart; refrigerate.

Raspberry Preserves

3. Carefully wash and drain the raspberries. Place in a saucepan, add the sugar and cook for 8 minutes. Set the raspberry preserves aside until completely cold.

Assembly

4. Preheat the oven to 340°F, 170°C or gas mark 3. Pour the raspberry preserves into the dough-lined tart pan; arrange the dough strips in a lattice pattern on the tart. Bake for 25 minutes. Remove the Linzertorte from the oven; serve when cold.

SPRING TWILIGHT BUFFET

· · ● · ·

Tomato *Mont-Blanc*

Lobster, Roasted Squash Seeds
and Salanova Salad

Steak and Caper Tartar, Gaufrette Potatoes

Wild Strawberry Tartlets

Mascarpone Sorbet

Melon Macarons

· · ● · ·

Mont-blanc à la tomate
Tomato Mont-Blanc

Serves 6
Preparation: 35 minutes

9 oz (250 g) yellow tomatoes
4½ oz (120 g) cocktail tomatoes
Salt, ground white pepper
1¼ cup (300 ml) heavy (double) cream, chilled
6 tsp dehydrated tomato flakes
6 sprigs chervil
Fleur de sel (sea salt crystals)
6 ladyfinger (*boudoir*) biscuits (optional)

Equipment
6 verrines, or stemmed glasses

1. Prepare a bowl of ice water. Bring a saucepan of water to the boil and immerse the yellow tomatoes for 10 seconds, transfer immediately to the ice water to cool; drain. Peel, seed and cut the yellow tomatoes into thin strips; season with salt and pepper. Quarter the cocktail tomatoes and scoop out the pulp.
2. Put the chilled cream into the bowl of an electric beater, season to taste with salt and pepper and whisk until light and airy but firm.
3. Half fill the verrines with the savoury whipped cream. Mound the yellow tomato strips in the centre of the whipped cream. Arrange the quartered tomatoes around each mound of yellow tomatoes. Decorate with tomato flakes and chervil sprigs. Sprinkle lightly with *fleur de sel*. Enjoy!

Chef's Tip
If you would like to give this dish a little more texture, crush the ladyfingers and put them into the bottom of the verrines.

Salade Salanova et homards aux graines de courge
Lobster, Roasted Squash Seeds and Salanova Salad

Serves 6
Preparation: 35 minutes
Cook: 3 minutes + 10 minutes

2 lb 10 oz (1.2 kg) live lobster
1 head salanova lettuce
2½ oz (60 g) squash seeds
1 tsp salt
2 tbsp (30 ml) white balsamic vinegar
½ tsp ground white pepper
¼ cup (60 ml) extra virgin olive oil

1. Put the lobster into a large saucepan of boiling water; cook for 3 minutes. Shell the lobster claws, arms and tails. Set the lobster meat aside.
2. Wash, spin-dry and set the salanova lettuce leaves aside in a damp tea (dish) towel.
3. Preheat the oven to 320°F, 160°C or gas mark 3. Spread the squash seeds out on a baking sheet. Roast in the oven for 7 minutes. Set aside until cold.
4. Put the salt into a bowl, add the white balsamic vinegar and whisk until the salt dissolves. Add the pepper and progressively whisk in the oil. Taste and adjust the seasonings if necessary. Set the vinaigrette aside.
5. Arrange the lettuce leaves on a platter, place the lobster meat on top and sprinkle with roasted squash seeds. Serve the vinaigrette on the side.

Chef's Tip
When choosing a live lobster, hold it behind the head and lift to make sure it still moves a little. The claws are usually held closed with a large elastic (rubber) band. Refrigerate the lobster uncovered in a deep dish. Never store a live lobster in a closed plastic bag...

Tartare de bœuf de Salers aux câpres de Pantelleria et pommes gaufrettes
Steak and Caper Tartar, Gaufrette Potatoes

Serves 6
Preparation: 35 minutes
Cook: 3 minutes

18 oz (500 g) salers beef
10½ oz (300 g) large potatoes
1 bunch green onions (scallions)
4 tsp finely sliced parsley leaves
4 tsp finely sliced cilantro (coriander) leaves
4 tsp finely sliced chives
2 tsp (12 g) Dijon mustard
2 organic egg yolks
1 tbsp (18 ml) ketchup
¾ tsp (3 ml) Worcestershire sauce
1 tbsp capers
Juice of 1 lemon
Salt, ground white pepper
Oil for frying
12 sprigs each parsley and cilantro
6 chives
Extra virgin olive oil

Equipment
1 mandolin

1. Trim the beef. Remove and discard excess fat and nerve tissue. Cut the beef into ¼ in (5 mm) dice; refrigerate until required.
2. Peel and slice the potatoes about ¹/₁₆ in (1 mm) thick using a mandolin equipped with the waffle blade; give the potato a ¼ turn after each cut. Put the slices immediately into a bowl of cold water until ready to deep fry.
3. Finely dice the green onions and set aside with the sliced parsley, cilantro and chives.
4. Put the mustard, egg yolks, ketchup and Worcestershire sauce into a bowl; whisk to combine. Add the diced beef, capers, green onions and sliced herbs; mix carefully. Sprinkle with lemon juice and season to taste with salt and pepper; refrigerate.
5. Fill a large saucepan or deep fryer no more than one-third full with oil and heat to 340°C (170°C). Drain and pat dry the sliced potatoes. Deep fry the potatoes in several batches until golden. Drain on a plate covered with kitchen paper, season immediately with salt.
6. Place a mound of the chilled beef tartar on each plate. Garnish with gaufrette potatoes. Decorate with the remaining herbs and drizzle with olive oil.

Chef's Tip

This dish is very easy to make, but be careful when using the mandolin which is an extremely sharp tool! The potatoes are finely sliced on mandolin equipped with a waffle blade. After each cut, the potato is given a ¼ turn to produce a waffled effect. Gaufrette or waffled potatoes are similar to potato chips. They can be served with an aperitif or used to garnish wild game or roasted poultry.

...

Tartelettes aux fraises des bois
Wild Strawberry Tartlets

Order this dessert from your local Ladurée patisserie.

Sorbet au mascarpone
Mascarpone Sorbet

Makes 1 quart (1 litre) sorbet
Preparation: 1 hour
Rest: 3 hours

½ organic or untreated lemon
1¼ cups water
1 cup (200 g) superfine (caster) sugar
7¾ oz (220 g) mascarpone
3½ tbsp (50 g) *fromage blanc* (fresh white cheese)

Equipment
Ice cream/sorbet machine (maker)

1. Zest the lemon using a vegetable peeler or citrus zester. Juice the lemon and set the juice aside.
2. Put the water, sugar and lemon zest into a saucepan and stir until the sugar dissolves. Bring to the boil and remove from the heat; infuse for 10 minutes. Strain the syrup and set aside until completely cold.
3. Put the mascarpone and *fromage blanc* into a bowl. Stir in the cold syrup and 1 tbsp of the lemon juice.
4. At least 3 hours before serving, pour the mixture into an ice cream machine and churn until soft and velvety.
5. Spoon the sorbet into a container and freeze until required. (The sorbet can be kept frozen for several days.) Remove the sorbet from the freezer 10 minutes before using to soften. Serve immediately.

Chef's Tip
This sorbet is even more delicious when served with the first wild strawberries of spring.

Macarons au melon
Melon Macarons

Order this dessert from your local Ladurée patisserie.

The Art of Entertaining

Setting the Stage
MAKE YOUR RECEPTION
A WORK OF ART

To create a beautiful setting with a unique atmosphere, pay careful attention to every detail. Play with different things such as the tableware, dishes to be served, colours and aromas. Don't hesitate to remove some of your usual decorating elements which might be better left to one side and which do not necessarily contribute to the spirit of the event. Often, it is better to downsize somewhat rather than add to the existing decor.

Expert Tip
CLEANING A WINE DECANTER

Decanter cleaning kits are available from wine accessories boutiques, hardware or even some department stores. They can also be purchased on the internet. You will need a long-handled decanter cleaning brush to remove tough stains. In any event, try not to leave tannic red wines too long in the decanter. Rinse it quickly with hot (not boiling) water after you have finished using it. And, never put the stopper in any decanter until it is completely dry.

A Touch of Folly
AN ORIGINAL CENTREPIECE

As early as the 18th Century, large tables or buffets were dressed with elaborate, decorative centrepieces of gilded bronze, silver, or porcelain. Some had candelabras for illuminating the table; others were also used holders or stands for cruet sets and a variety of condiments such as salt, pepper, mustard, etc. Today these centrepieces are found in museums or top-notch antique stores. However, it is still an important part of the decor to have a centre focal point, either classic or spectacular, on a buffet table. A pyramid of exotic fruit could well play this role. Why not consider a tiered cake, a tall bouquet of greenery, or even a taxidermy bird under a glass dome…?

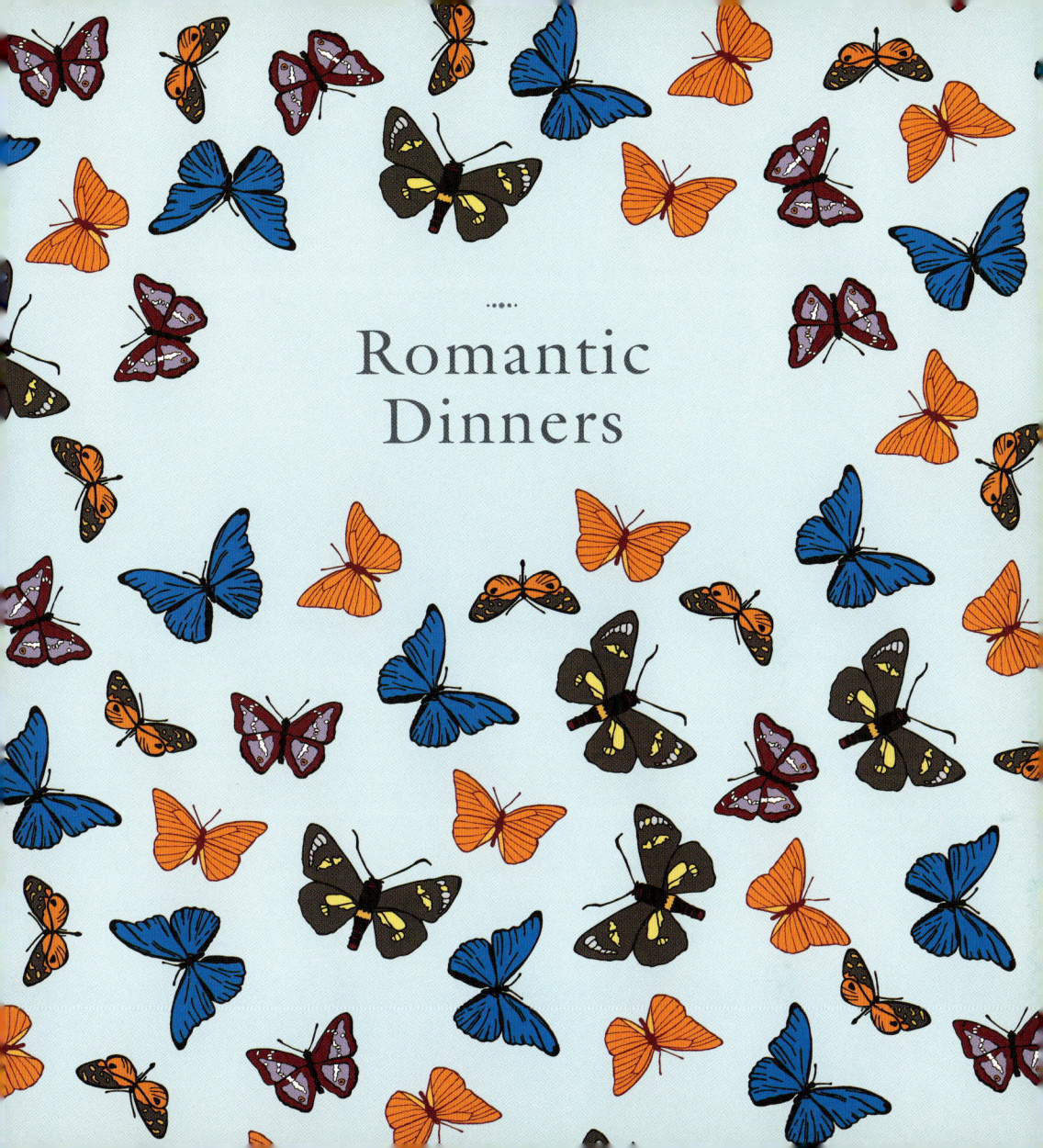
Romantic Dinners

ALLURING DINNER

Choux Puffs with Eggplant Caviar and Kalamata Olives

Crab-Filled Avocado Cannelloni

John Dory Fillets with Apples and Jasmine Cream

Kirsch-Flamed Cherries, Pistachio Ice Cream

Rose Nougat

Mon petit chou à l'aubergine et olives de Kalamata

Choux Puffs with Eggplant Caviar and Kalamata Olives

Serves 2
Preparation: 35 minutes
Cook: 25 minutes + 1 hour

Choux Pastry
⅓ cup + 1 tsp (40 g) cake flour
3 tbsp + 1 tsp (50 ml) water
7 tsp (35 g) butter
1 pinch salt
2 eggs
Softened butter for the baking sheet
1 egg + 1 pinch salt, beaten for glazing

Eggplant Caviar
2 cloves garlic, sliced
1 large eggplant (aubergine)
3 tbsp (45 ml) olive oil
1½ tsp salt
1 tsp (2 g) pepper

Assembly
Fleur de sel (sea salt crystals)
Fresh thyme leaves
2 large black Kalamata olives, quartered

Equipment
Piping bag fitted with a ⅜ in (10 mm) tip

Choux Pastry
1. Preheat the oven to 355°F, 180°C or gas mark 4. Sift the flour. Put the water, butter and salt into a saucepan and bring to the boil; remove from the heat immediately. Tip all the sifted flour into the hot liquid. Beat vigorously with a wooden spoon until a thick, smooth dough forms. Return the saucepan to low heat and continue beating for 1 minute to dry the dough. Remove from the heat and place the dough in a bowl. Add the eggs one by one, beating well after each addition until the dough is smooth, shiny and falls in a point from the spoon. Do not allow it to become too liquid.
2. Spoon the dough into the piping bag fitted with the ⅜ in (10 mm) tip. Lightly brush a baking sheet with the softened butter and pipe mounds of dough onto it. Bake 25 minutes, or until dry and golden. Cool the choux puffs on a rack.

Eggplant Caviar
3. Lower the oven temperature to 340°F, 170°C or gas mark 3. Wash and cut the ends off the eggplant. Then, cut it lengthwise in half and incise the flesh with the point of a small knife being careful not to pierce the skin. Gently push the sliced garlic into the incisions, sprinkle the flesh with olive oil and season with salt and pepper. Wrap the eggplant halves in aluminium

(tin) foil. Cook in the oven for 1 hour. Use a spoon to scoop the cooked flesh out of the eggplants and chop to a coarse puree. Set the eggplant caviar aside until cold; taste and adjust the seasonings.

Assembly

4. Spoon the eggplant caviar into the piping bag fitted with the tip. Make a lengthwise incision in the tops of the choux puffs. Pipe the eggplant caviar generously into each one. Decorate with Kalamata olive quarters and thyme leaves; sprinkle with *fleur de sel*.

Chef's Tip

If you wish to keep the eggplant caviar for a few days, cover with a very thin layer of olive oil and refrigerate it. Olives are on every table nowadays and there is a wide range available; Greek Kalamata olives are perhaps the most famous. They are smooth skinned, fleshy, greenish violet in colour with a slightly vinegary taste.

Cannelloni « amoreto » au tourteau et à l'avocat
Crab-Filled Avocado Cannelloni

Serves 2
Preparation: 25 minutes

1½ oz (40 g) crab meat
½ tsp sesame seeds
1 tsp finely sliced tarragon leaves
Salt, ground white pepper
1 avocado (not too ripe)
4 tsp (20 ml) lemon juice
2 tsp (10 ml) extra virgin olive oil
Fleur de sel (sea salt crystals)

1. Shred the crab meat and place in a bowl. Add the sesame seeds and tarragon; season to taste with salt and pepper.
2. Cut the avocado carefully in half and remove the pit (stone). Cut the flesh into paper thin slices. Put a piece of plastic (cling) wrap onto a work surface. Lay the avocado slices on it to form a rectangle. Brush with lemon juice and season with salt, pepper.

3. Spoon the seasoned crab meat along short edge of the avocado rectangle. Using the plastic wrap as a guide, slowly pull up the edge, and roll the avocado over to form it into a cannelloni shape.

4. Put the cannelloni into the freezer for a few minutes to firm; cut it into segments, remove and discard the plastic wrap. Place the cannelloni segments on a plate, drizzle with olive oil; sprinkle with fleur de sel.

Blanc de saint-pierre au jasmin et pomme d'amour

John Dory Fillets with Apples and Jasmine Cream

Serves 2
Preparation: 25 minutes
Cook: 25 minutes

1 cup (250 ml) water
½ tsp coarse salt
1 tsp finely chopped ginger root
1 teaspoon finely chopped lemon grass
5 tsp jasmine tea leaves
2½ tbsp (50 ml) heavy (double) cream
6¼ oz (180 g) apples
2 tbsp (30 g) butter
Salt, ground white pepper

2 John Dory fillets, 6 oz (160 g) each
4 tsp (20 ml) extra virgin olive oil
Green shiso sprouts
Fleur de sel (sea salt crystals)

1. Put the water, coarse salt, ginger and lemon grass into a saucepan. Simmer for 10 minutes. Remove from the heat, add the jasmine tea and infuse for 10 minutes. Stir in the cream and return the saucepan to the heat; simmer for 5 minutes. Use a fine wire mesh strainer to strain the mixture. Set the jasmine cream aside to keep warm.

2. Peel, core and quarter the apples. Put the butter into a frying pan over low heat. Add the apples and cook gently until lightly golden; season to taste with salt and pepper. Set aside.

3. Preheat the oven to 300°F, 150°C or gas mark 2. Place the John Dory fillets in an ovenproof pan, sprinkle with the olive oil and season with salt and pepper. Cook in the oven for 8 minutes.

4. Arrange the apples on the plates and place a John Dory fillet on each one. Just before serving, emulsify the jasmine cream sauce using a stick blender. Nap the fish with the sauce. Decorate with green shiso sprouts. Sprinkle with *fleur de sel*.

Fricassée de cerises et crème glacée à la pistache
Kirsch-Flamed Cherries, Pistachio Ice Cream

Serves 2
Preparation: 2 hours 15 minutes
Cook: 25 minutes

Cherry Juice
18 oz (500 g) cherries, pitted (stoned)
3 tbsp (45 g) superfine (caster) sugar

Kirsch-Flamed Cherries
14 oz (400 g) cherries
1 tbsp (15 g) unsalted butter
2½ tbsp (30 g) superfine (caster) sugar
3 tbsp (45 ml) cherry juice
1 tbsp (15 ml) kirsch (cherry brandy)

Assembly
1 qt (1 L) pistachio ice cream

CHERRY JUICE
1. Cut the pitted cherries in halves and place in bowl; add the sugar. Cook in a *bain-marie* (water bath) over low heat for 25 minutes, to obtain a sweet juice. Strain and set the juice aside.

KIRSCH-FLAMED CHERRIES
2. Carefully wash and cut the cherries into halves using a small knife; remove the pit (stone). Melt the butter in a small sauté pan and sprinkle with sugar. Add the cherries and cook for 2 to 3 minutes over very high heat. Stir in the cherry juice, add the kirsch and flame. Allow the kirsch-cherry sauce to reduce for 1 minute; set aside to keep warm.

ASSEMBLY
3. Remove the pistachio ice cream from the freezer to soften for 10 minutes before serving. Spoon the cherries onto two plates, nap with the sauce and place a scoop of pistachio ice cream on top of the warm cherries. Serve immediately.

Chef's Tip
If you have a small heart-shaped cake tart ring or pan with a removable bottom, put it on the plate, spoon the cherries into it, nap with the sauce, put the ice cream on top and carefully slide off the mould.

Variation
Adapt this recipe for strawberries served with coconut ice cream: Wash and quarter 14 oz (400 g) of strawberries. Melt 1 tbsp (15 g) butter in a pan. Add the strawberries, sprinkle with 2½ tbsp (30 g) sugar and cook for 3 to 4 minutes. Stir in 1 tbsp (15 ml) balsamic vinegar. Serve the strawberries with a scoop of coconut ice cream.

Nougat à la rose
Rose Nougat

Makes 3¼ lbs (1.5 kg) nougat
Preparation: 1 hour
Cook: 25 minutes

Rose Nougat
13¼ oz (375 g) whole blanched almonds
2 scant cups (370 g) superfine (caster) sugar
¾ cup (180 g) liquid glucose
¾ cup (180 ml) water
¾ cup (250 g) honey
2 egg whites
7 oz (200 g) candied (crystallised) rose petals
3 tbsp (45 ml) rose syrup

Assembly
2 sheets edible rice (wafer) paper

Equipment
Electric stand mixer (whisk + flat beater)
2 digital thermometers

ROSE NOUGAT

1. Preheat the oven to 285°F, 140°C or gas mark 1. Cover a baking sheet with baking parchment and put the almonds onto it. Roast for 10 minutes then, turn off and leave the almonds in the oven to keep warm.

2. Put the sugar, glucose and water into a saucepan. Pour the honey into a separate saucepan. Put the egg whites into the bowl of the mixer and whisk very slowly until firm. Cook the sugar-water-glucose mixture until it reaches a temperature of 239°F (115° C).

3. At the same time, cook the honey until it reaches a temperature of 248°F (120°C); continue cooking until the temperature is 275°F (135°C). Remove from the heat immediately and carefully pour the honey into the egg whites with the mixer running.

4. Continue cooking the sugar-water-glucose mixture until it is 293° F (145°C) then, pour it into the egg white mixture as described above. Reduce the speed of the mixer and whisk for 5 minutes.

5. Replace the whisk with a flat beater. Add the warm almonds, crystallised rose petals and the rose syrup; beat on high speed for 30 seconds.

Assembly

6. Pour the nougat onto one of the rice paper sheets. With wet hands, tap the nougat into an even shape and cover with the remaining rice paper. Set aside until cold. Cut the nougat into the desired shapes.

The Art of Entertaining

Setting the Stage

CREATE A SERENE ATMOSPHERE

For an intimate, romantic dinner, avoid using lots of very bright lighting. On the contrary, such dinners are to be enjoyed by candlelight, or light from subtle, discreetly placed table lamps. Choose peaceful music that will last for quite a while... There is nothing worse than having to get up from the table to change a CD. And, don't forget the flowers...a simple rose resting on the napkin (serviette) or plate is already a tender invitation.

Table Etiquette

THE ART OF FINGER BOWLS

The use of finger bowls has become a rather lost art. However, they are appreciated especially when seafood, for example, is being served. Prepare a small bowl for each guest. Put a little warm or cold water (depending on the season) into each one and add a slice of lemon or lime. For an extra touch, float mint leaves or a small flower, such as a daisy, or a hortensia floret, on the surface of the water.

Tableware

PUT UTENSILS
IN THE CORRECT ORDER

Hors d'oeuvres, fish or meat courses... what is the correct order of the utensils? As a general rule, they are placed on the table in order of use, starting at the outside for the first course to be served and working inwards to the plate. It is best to limit the number of utensils on the table, with a maximum of three on each side of the plate. Cheese knives, cake forks and small spoons are only set out on the table at informal meals. However, in France, the fork tines or spoon rims are placed on the table touching the cloth. The British or American presentation is generally the opposite. As far as knives are concerned, the cutting side of the blade is always turned towards the plate.

the baking sheet. Leave sufficient space between the piped fingers because they will spread during cooking. Bake for 10 to 12 minutes until golden. Remove from the oven, and cool slightly.
Use a spatula to lift the cat's tongues off the baking parchment; cool on a rack and store in an airtight container until required.

3. Tempering chocolate is fairly technical but here is a simple method: Chop the chocolate on a cutting board. Put the chopped chocolate in a bowl and melt over a slowly simmering *bain-marie* (water bath) until smooth. Pour ¾ of the chocolate onto a clean, dry work surface. Use an offset metal spatula and work the chocolate in a back and forth motion, until it starts to thicken. Put the thickened chocolate into the bowl containing the remaining melted chocolate and gently stir until evenly blended. Tempered chocolate must be used when it is 86 to 87.8° F (30 to 31°C). If the chocolate is too hot or too cold, it will whiten as it cools and loose its shine.

4. Dip the cat's tongues into the tempered chocolate and set aside to harden; store in an airtight container.

Chef's Tip
Serve the chocolate cat's tongues with a caramel mousse or a coffee.

Vacherin au citron et citron confit
Lemon Vacherin with Candied Lemons

Serves 2
Preparation: 2 hours 15 minutes
Cook: 6 minutes + 2 hours 30 minutes
Freeze: 3 hours

Candied Lemons
2 organic or untreated lemons
⅔ cup water (150 ml) water
7 tbsp (100 ml) lemon juice
½ cup (100 g) superfine (caster) sugar

Meringue
1 cup (120 g) confectioner's (icing) sugar
4 egg whites
½ cup + 2 tbsp (120 g) superfine (caster) sugar

Lemon Sorbet
4 organic or untreated lemons
1¾ cups + 1 tbsp (450 ml) water
2½ tbsp (20 g) powdered milk
1½ cups (300 g) superfine (caster) sugar
¾ cup + 2 tbsp (200 ml) lemon juice, chilled

Equipment
Piping bag fitted with a 5/16 in (8 mm) plain tip
Ice cream/sorbet machine (maker)
2 small heart shaped tart (pastry) rings

CANDIED LEMONS

1. Cut the lemons into slices ⅛ in (3 mm) thick. Put the slices into a saucepan, fill with cold water and bring to the boil; drain. Repeat this operation once.
2. Put the blanched lemon slices into a small sauté pan. Add the water, lemon juice and ¼ cup (50 g) of the sugar. Simmer for 3 minutes then remove from the heat. Add 2 tbsp (25 g) of the sugar and set aside. When cold, return the pan to the heat, simmer for 3 minutes, remove from the heat, add the remaining sugar and set aside.

MERINGUE

3. Preheat the oven to 210°F, 100°C or gas mark less than ¼. Cover a baking sheet with baking parchment. Sift the confectioner's sugar and set aside.
4. Put the egg whites into a bowl and whisk until frothy. Add 3 tbsp (40 g) of the superfine sugar a little at a time and whisk until the egg whites are firm. Add another 3 tbsp (40 g) of the sugar and whisk for 1 minute. Add the remaining sugar and whisk for another minute. Use a spatula to gently fold in the sifted confectioner's sugar.
5. Spoon the meringue into the piping bag and pipe small fingers of meringue onto the baking sheet. Bake for 2½ hours; do not allow the meringues to colour too quickly. They must cook slowly and be dry when cooked. Set aside until cold.

LEMON SORBET

6. Zest the lemons using a fine grater. Put the water, powdered milk, sugar and lemon zest into a saucepan and bring to the boil; remove from the heat. When cold, add the lemon juice. At least 3 hours before serving, pour the mixture into an ice cream machine and churn until soft and velvety. Spoon the sorbet into a container and freeze until required. (It can be made in advance and kept frozen for several days.) Remove the sorbet from the freezer 10 minutes before using to soften.

ASSEMBLY

7. Fill two heart shaped pastry rings with lemon sorbet and unmold one on each plate. Decorate with candied lemon slices and meringue fingers. Enjoy!

Variation

Here are some other variations you could consider for this recipe: raspberry-rose petal sorbet with rose meringue; sour cherry-pistachio sorbet with pistachio meringue; pineapple-lemon sorbet with coconut meringue; chocolate-kumquat sorbet with cocoa meringue…

INTIMATE DINNER

· · ● · ·

Goose *Foie Gras* Dressed in Red and Black

Sea Bass Tartar with Pink Grapefruit

Veal with Truffle Ravioli

A Citrus Heart to Share

Soft Chocolate-Macadamia Caramels

· · ● · ·

Foie gras d'oie en rouge et noir

Goose Foie Gras Dressed in Red and Black

Serves 2
Preparation: 45 minutes
Cook: 20 minutes
Refrigerate: 12 hours minimum

Goose Foie Gras
18 oz (500 g) fresh goose *foie gras*
Salt, ground white pepper
3 cherry macarons

Black Cream
3½ tbsp (50 ml) heavy (double) cream
½ tsp (2 g) squid ink
Salt, ground white pepper

Assembly
1 Ladurée cherry macaron
Fleur de sel (sea salt crystals)
Finely sliced fresh truffles (optional)
2 slices Ladurée kugelhopf (challah) toasted (opt.)

Goose Foie Gras

1. Prepare the *foie gras* at least 12 hours before serving. Crush the cherry macarons between two sheets of baking parchment; set aside. Devein the *foie gras* and season with one teaspoon each of salt and pepper. Cut the foie gras lengthwise into two equal portions. Spread one portion in the bottom of a terrine and cover with a thin layer of the crushed macarons. Put the remaining *foie gras* on top, press firmly to smooth the surface.
2. Preheat the oven to 210°F, 100°C or gas mark less than ¼. Prepare a container of crushed ice. Fill a baking dish with hot water and put the terrine of *foie gras* into it. Transfer to the oven and cook for 20 minutes. Remove from the oven and stand the terrine in the crushed ice to cool. Refrigerate for at least 12 hours.

Black Cream

3. Pour the cream into a saucepan and reduce over low heat until thickened. Stir in the squid ink, season to taste with salt and pepper; set aside to keep warm.

Assembly

4. Cut the cherry macaron in half. Cut two slices* from the *foie gras*, ⅝ in (15 mm) thick. Put one on each plate and top with a macaron half. Spoon ribbons of black cream around the *foie gras* and sprinkle with *fleur de sel*.
5. If desired, decorate with truffle slices and serve with toasted kugelhopf.

Chef's Tip

*Store the left-over foie gras, in an airtight container. It can be kept for up to 3 days. Also, note that French or Hungarian goose foie gras is milder than duck foie gras.

Un amour de bar mariné au pamplemousse
Sea Bass Tartar with Pink Grapefruit

Serves 2
Preparation: 15 minutes

7 oz (200 g) centre-cut sea bass fillet
1 green Thai mango
1 bright green stalk celery
1 pink grapefruit
2 tbsp (30 ml) extra virgin olive oil
Salt, ground white pepper
2 tsp finely sliced fresh tarragon leaves
Parmesan cheese shavings
Fleur de sel (sea salt crystals)

1. Cut the sea bass fillet into $1/8$ in (3 mm) dice and refrigerate. Peel the mango. Finely dice the mango and celery; set aside.
2. Use a small sharp knife to cut off all the grapefruit skin without leaving any pith. Working over a bowl to recuperate the juice, insert the knife between the grapefruit segments and the membrane. Cut out all the segments without any membrane; refrigerate until required. Strain the juice into a small bowl, season to taste with salt and pepper and whisk in the olive oil. Set the pink grapefruit sauce aside.
3. Put the diced sea bass, mango and celery into a bowl; season to taste with salt and pepper. Pour the sauce over the sea bass mixture; gently stir in the tarragon.
4. Mound the sea bass tartar on two plates. Decorate with pink grapefruit segments and Parmesan shavings; dust with *fleur de sel*.

Princesse de veau et tendres ravioles à la truffe
Veal with Truffle Ravioli

Serves 2
Preparation: 25 minutes
Cook: 1 hour 20 minutes

Veal Jus
12½ oz (350 g) eye round (topside) veal
1 small onion, diced
1 carrot, diced
1 tomato, diced
1 tbsp fresh thyme leaves
Salt, ground white pepper

Truffle Ravioli
1 small carrot, diced
1½ oz (40 g) zucchini (courgette), diced
1½ oz (40 g) celery root (celeriac), diced
3½ oz (100 g) small white mushrooms
1 tbsp (15 ml) extra virgin olive oil
⅜ oz (10 g) black truffle, crushed
10 ravioli dough sheets (wonton wrappers)

Veal
Salt, ground white pepper
2 tbsp (30 ml) extra virgin olive oil
4 tsp (20 g) butter

Assembly
⅜ oz (10 g) black truffle, finely sliced
4 chervil sprigs
Fleur de sel (sea salt crystals)

Veal Jus

1. Trim and cut the veal into two equal portions. Set the trimmings aside. Refrigerate the veal.
2. Preheat the oven to 355°F, 180°C or gas mark 4. Chop the veal trimmings and place in a roasting pan. Roast until browned, about 15 minutes. Add the onion, carrot, tomato and thyme leaves and continue roasting for a few more minutes.
3. Pour the contents of the roasting pan into a saucepan. Add cold water to cover, bring to the boil and cook over medium heat for 50 minutes. Strain into a bowl, return the stock to a saucepan and reduce over low heat to obtain a slightly syrupy *jus*; season to taste with salt and pepper if necessary. Set the veal *jus* aside to keep warm.

Truffle Ravioli

4. Prepare a bowl of ice water. Cook the diced vegetables separately in boiling salted water, drain and refresh in iced water; drain again. Cook the carrot and celery for 2 minutes; the zucchini for 1 minute. Rinse, dry and quarter the mushrooms. Heat the olive oil in a frying pan. Cook the mushrooms for 5 minutes; season with salt and pepper. Put all the vegetables into a bowl and add the crushed truffle. Carefully stir to combine all the filling ingredients.
5. Place one ravioli dough sheet on a work surface or cutting board and put a spoonful of the filling in the centre. Brush the exposed dough lightly with water and fold it on the diagonal to form a triangle; press down well on the edges to seal. Repeat to make 10 ravioli. Put the ravioli onto a plate, cover with plastic (cling) wrap and refrigerate.

Veal

6. Preheat the oven to 355°F, 180°C or gas mark 4. Season the veal with salt and pepper. Heat the olive oil in an ovenproof frying pan over high heat. Add the veal portions and brown quickly and evenly. Dot the veal with small pieces of the butter. Finish cooking in the oven for 6 minutes. Remove from the oven, cover with tin (aluminium) foil and set aside to keep warm.

Assembly

7. Bring a large saucepan of salted water to the boil. Immerse the ravioli one by one.

Cook 2 – 3 minutes until they float up to the surface; drain.

8. Put 5 ravioli and a veal portion on each plate; spoon the *jus* over the veal. Decorate with sliced truffle and sprigs of chervil. Sprinkle with *fleur de sel*. Enjoy.

Chef's Tip
If you prefer crispy ravioli, you could reheat them in a frying pan with a little olive oil.

Un cœur pour deux aux agrumes
A Citrus Heart to Share

Serves 2
Preparation: 20 minutes
Cook: 10 minutes + 15 minutes
Rest: 12 hours
Refrigerate: 1 hour

Almond Sweet Pastry
½ cup + 1 tbsp (70g) confectioner's (icing) sugar
1¾ cups (200 g) cake flour
8 tbsp or 4¼ oz (120 g) unsalted butter, chilled
¼ cup (25 g) ground almonds (almond flour)
Pinch *fleur de sel* (sea salt crystals)
1 egg
Butter softened, for the tart pan
Flour for work surface

Honey Almond Cream
7 tbsp (100 g) butter
¼ cup (100 g) honey
1 cup (100 g) ground almonds (almond flour)
5 tsp (10 g) cornstarch (cornflour)
2 eggs, beaten

Citrus Fruit
1 organic or untreated orange
1 organic or untreated pink grapefruit
Zest of 1 organic or untreated lime

Equipment
1 heart-shaped tart ring/pan (removable bottom)
Dried beans
1 piping bag fitted with a ⅜ in (10 mm) tip

ALMOND SWEET PASTRY
1. Sift the confectioner's sugar and the flour separately. Cut the butter into small pieces and place in a bowl. Cream the butter using a wooden spoon, or place it in an upright mixer equipped with a flat beater. Blend in the following ingredients one by one: the confectioner's sugar, ground almonds, salt, egg and then, the flour. Mix until the ingredients just start to stick together. Roll the dough into a ball, flatten and wrap in plastic (cling) wrap; refrigerate for 12 hours. (If the dough is overworked, the texture of the cooked pastry will not be crisp and crunchy.)

2. Butter the tart pan. Dust the work surface with flour. Roll the dough out evenly to a thickness of $^1/_{16}$ in (2 mm) and line the tart pan with it. Refrigerate for 1 hour.

3. Preheat the oven to 340°F, 170°C or gas mark 3. Prick the dough with a fork so it will remain flat during cooking. Cut out a 12 in (30 cm) disc of baking parchment. Carefully place the parchment disc in the dough lined pan, pressing it well into the angles. Fill with dried beans to hold the parchment in place during cooking.
4. Bake for about 10 minutes and remove from the oven. The dough will only be half-cooked; set aside until cold. Do not turn off the oven.

Honey Almond Cream
5. Cut the butter into small pieces and place in a bowl over a slowly simmering *bain-marie* (water bath). Beat until the butter is thick and creamy but not melted. One by one, and whisking thoroughly after each addition, add the honey, ground almonds, cornstarch and eggs.
6. Spoon the cream into the piping bag. Pipe it into the tart shell, to come to the half-way mark. Bake in the preheated oven for 15 minutes. Remove and set the tart aside until completely cold.

Citrus Fruit
7. Use a small sharp knife to cut off all the orange and pink grapefruit skin without leaving any of the white pith. Insert the knife between the flesh and the membrane and cut out all the segments. Zest the lime using a fine grater.

Arrange the citrus fruit segments harmoniously on the tart. Scatter the lime zest over the top. Enjoy!

Chef's Tip
If you have some orange marmalade on hand, spread it on the inner surface of the tart shell, pour the honey almond cream on top and bake.

Caramels mous au chocolat et macadamia
Soft Chocolate-Macadamia Caramels

Order this dessert from your local Ladurée patisserie.

The Art of Entertaining

Setting the Stage
FLAVOURS AND TEXTURES
TO CHARM THE SENSES

Flavours and textures of a meal are important but often overlooked details. Smooth and creamy goose *foie gras*, melt-in-the-mouth marinated sea bass, small ravioli tender as a kiss, and the caramel's soft sensuality, all conjure up a subliminal image or hidden message of love and pleasure!

Savoir-Faire
SWEETMEATS
IN THE SITTING ROOM

To extend the enjoyment of dessert, serve the coffee with some small sweetmeats such as rose macarons, chocolate-coated almonds, sugar-coated fruit... Since only two of you will be sharing the romantic dinner, choose tiny, easily served items in small liqueur glasses, little saucers, coffee spoons, verrines... Keep in mind that Japanese tableware has a wide range of very small recipients, mini-bowls and saucers, all in translucent porcelain. Their transparency and finesse will also contribute to the subtle charm of the moment.

A Question of Style
A WINE DECANTER

Serve the wine in a pretty crystal decanter at your 'dinner for two', not for the usual reasons, which are to aerate a young wine or decant a prestigious vintage, but rather to give you the opportunity to serve the wine elegantly, and to let the room's soft lighting emphasize the decanter's curves...

Winter Suppers

COUNTRY SUPPER

· · ● · ·

Country-Style Duck Pâtés in Puff Pastry

Pike-Perch with Grape-Red Wine Preserves
and Forgotten Vegetables

Caramelised Autumn Fruit, Spiced *Arlettes*

· · ● · ·

Pâtés en croûte de nos campagnes

Country-Style Duck Pâtés in Puff Pastry

Serves 4
Preparation: 40 minutes
Cook: 55 minutes
Rest: 45 minutes

Duck Pâté
3 oz (80 g) duck *foie gras*
3½ oz (100 g) duck breast
1 oz (30 g) poultry livers
2 tbsp (30 ml) extra virgin olive oil
4 tsp finely sliced sage leaves
4 tsp finely sliced rosemary leaves
7 oz (200 g) duck leg meat, chopped
2 tsp (10 g) duck fat
2 tsp salt
2 tsp ground white pepper

Puff Pastry Cases
8 discs puff pastry dough, 4¾ in (12 cm)
2 eggs, beaten

Assembly
½ cup (120 ml) Maggi® aspic jelly

Equipment
4 individual pâté moulds, 4 in (10 cm) diameter

Duck Pâté
1. Cut the foie gras and the duck breast into ⅜ in (10 mm) dice. Cut the poultry livers into ¾ in (20 mm) dice. Put the olive oil in a frying pan over high heat. Add the diced duck breast and poultry livers, pan fry for 2 minutes; drain.
2. Put the duck breast and livers into a bowl. Add the sage and rosemary, the *foie gras*, duck leg meat and fat; season with salt and pepper and mix carefully to combine all the ingredients.

Puff Pastry Cases
3. Preheat the oven to 355°F, 180°C or gas mark 4. Line a mould with a puff pastry disc. Put a quarter of the pâté mixture into the lined mould. Brush a ¾ in (20 mm) border of beaten egg on one of the puff pastry discs. Put it on top of the pâté mixture. Carefully insert the overhanging puff pastry into the mould to cover the puff pastry liner, forming a perfect seal. Repeat for the remaining 3 moulds.
3. Bake in the preheated oven for 30 minutes. Reduce the oven temperature to 300°F, 150°C or gas mark 2 and continue baking for 25 minutes.

Assembly
4. When the pâtés are cold, make a ⅜ in (10 mm) hole in the bases and fill with the aspic. Set aside to rest for 45 minutes before serving.

Sandre glacé au vin rouge et légumes oubliés

Pike-Perch with Grape-Red Wine Preserves and Forgotten Vegetables

Serves 4
Preparation: 45 minutes
Cook: 20 minutes

4½ oz (125 g) purple carrots
4½ oz (125 g) crapaudine beets (beetroots)
4½ oz (125 g) parsnips
4½ oz (125 g) rutabaga (swede)
5¼ oz (150 g) golden delicious apples
7 oz (200 g) black grapes
2 cups (500 ml) red wine (11%)
¼ cup (50 g) granulated sugar
4 thick pieces pike-perch fillet (skin on),
  5¼ oz (150 g) each
Salt, ground white pepper
3½ tbsp (50 ml) extra virgin olive oil
4 tsp (20 g) butter
Fleur de sel (sea salt crystals)

---

1. Wash, peel and cut the vegetables into pieces. Prepare a bowl of chilled water and crushed ice. Cook the vegetables separately in boiling water until soft; drain. Refresh in the chilled water to stop the cooking and drain again; set aside.

2. Wash, peel and finely dice the apples. Quarter the grapes and place in a saucepan. Add the red wine, sugar and apples. Simmer the mixture over low heat until thickened; set the grape-red wine preserves aside.

3. Season the pike-perch pieces with salt and pepper. Heat the olive oil in a frying pan. Put the fish into the pan, skin-side down and lightly brown. Turn and cook the other side over low heat until golden.

4. Put the butter in a frying pan, add all the vegetables and reheat gently.

5. Arrange the vegetables decoratively on plates. Put a spoonful of grape-red wine preserves on each one and top with the fish, skin side up. Dust lightly with *fleur de sel*. Enjoy!

Chef's Tip

The pike-perch is a freshwater fish. Its delicate white flesh is quite firm and lean with few bones. Usually farmed, this fish is available all year round, either whole or filleted. The "forgotten vegetables" are not really as forgotten as it seems! They are vegetables used by our fore bearers and revived today by chefs. The ones proposed in this recipe (rutabagas and parsnips, etc.) can be replaced with others in the winter, depending on product availability.

Fruits d'automne rôtis et arlettes épicées
Caramelised Autumn Fruit, Spiced Arlettes

Serves 4
Preparation: 30 minutes
Cook: 15 minutes
Rest: Overnight

Spiced Arlettes
¾ cup + 1 tbsp (100 g) confectioner's (icing) sugar
2½ tsp ground cinnamon
1¼ tsp ground star anise
3½ oz (100 g) puff pastry dough

Caramelised Autumn Fruit
1 boskoop apple
1 bosc pear
½ quince
4½ oz (125 g) black grapes
4½ oz (125 g) white grapes
2 tbsp (30 g) unsalted butter
3 tbsp (40 g) superfine (caster) sugar
Juice of 1 lemon
7 tbsp (100 ml) apple juice

SPICED ARLETTES

1. Combine the confectioner's sugar and spices. Sprinkle the sugar mixture little by little onto the puff pastry while rolling it out to a thickness of ¹⁄₁₆ in (2 mm). Use a cutter to stamp out 1¼ in (3 cm) discs of dough. Set aside uncovered to dry overnight.

2. Preheat the oven 390°F, 200°C or gas mark 6. Put the *arlettes* on a non-stick baking sheet and bake for 7 minutes until smooth and caramelised; cool. Store the *arlettes* in an airtight container.

CARAMELISED AUTUMN FRUIT

3. Wash all the fruit. Cut the apple and pear into eighths and set aside. Peel and finely slice the quince. Remove the grapes from the stems.

4. Put the butter in a frying pan over medium heat. When it foams, add the sugar and cook until caramelised. Deglaze the pan with the lemon juice. Lower the heat and carefully place the fruit in the caramel; little by little, add half the apple juice.

5. Cook the apple and pear for 5 minutes and remove from the pan. Continue cooking the quince and grapes for 3 minutes; remove from the pan. Add the remaining apple juice to the caramelised cooking liquid and reduce the sauce until slightly thickened.

ASSEMBLY

6. Arrange the fruit decoratively on plates, nap with the caramelised sauce and place 3 *arlettes* on each serving. Serve immediately.

The Art of Entertaining

Savoir-Faire

FROM WHICH SIDE DO WE SERVE?

Platters or dressed plates are always presented or served on the right-hand side of the guest. They are removed from the table on the guest's left-hand side.
Also, for the salad and cheese courses, second helpings are not usually offered.

Table Etiquette

THE BREAD

Serve the bread already sliced or cut on the diagonal into larger pieces. Place it in a bread basket lined with a folded linen napkin (serviette). If possible, do not leave the basket on the table but, rather, on a side table. The bread is placed to the left of the plate, either on a small bread plate or directly on the tablecloth. It is considered bad form to roll the soft dough of your bread into balls! To eat it, simply tear off small pieces by hand. After the cheese has been served, the host will discretely sweep up the crumbs.

Expert Tip

CARING FOR SILVERWARE

There are all types of products on the market for cleaning silverware.
Make your own using a paste of baking soda and water, or use the cooking liquid from spinach or potatoes. Whatever method used, always buff the silver with a soft cloth after cleaning. Choose a dark, dry storage place for your silver. You could even make protective flannel bags for your flatware; wrap large platters in dark tissue paper. These precautions will all help to prevent tarnishing.

PARISIAN SUPPER

Cream of Red Hubbard Squash
and Almond Soup

Honeyed Capon in Fig Leaves, Potato Croquettes

Chestnut Macarons

Chocolate-Orange Delight

Crème de potimarron à l'amande

Cream of Red Hubbard Squash and Almond Soup

Serves 4
Preparation: 20 minutes
Cook: 1 hour

---

1 lb 12 oz (800 g) red hubbard (onion) squash
3 oz (80 g) onion
4 tsp (20 ml) extra virgin olive oil
¾ cup (200 ml) heavy (double) cream
1 large pinch nutmeg
Salt, ground white pepper
1 tbsp (10 g) almond cream
2 tbsp (10 g) sliced almonds

---

1. Peel, seed and coarsely chop the squash. Peel and dice the onion. Heat the olive oil in a saucepan, add the onions and cook gently without colouring for 2 minutes. Add the squash and heavy cream and cook for 5 minutes. Add water to barely cover the squash and season with the nutmeg, and salt and pepper to taste; simmer over low heat for 1 hour.
2. Place a colander over a bowl to recuperate the cooking liquid. Drain the cooked squash and place in the bowl of a food processor; pulse to a puree, adding the cooking liquid as necessary. Add the almond paste and process to obtain a thick, creamy soup.
3. Preheat the oven to 320F, 160°C or gas mark 3. Spread the sliced almonds on a baking sheet and roast in the oven for 7 minutes, or until golden.
4. Serve in a soup tureen and sprinkle with roasted almonds.

Chef's Tip

A red hubbard squash has been used for this recipe. However, it could be prepared with a variety of other squash including, pumpkin, butternut, acorn...

Chapon au miel de pin et feuille de figuier

Honeyed Capon in Fig Leaves, Potato Croquettes

Serves 4
Preparation: 40 minutes
Cook: 55 minutes

20 oz (600 g) potatoes
Coarse salt
Salt, ground white pepper
½ cup (60 g) all purpose (plain) flour
2 eggs, beaten
½ cup (60 g) breadcrumbs
1 dressed capon, 4½ lbs (2 kg)
1 tbsp (10 g) fresh thyme leaves
1 bay leaf
1½ tbsp (30 g) pine honey
2 large fig leaves
Oil for frying

1. Preheat the oven to 340°F, 170°C or gas mark 3. Wash and prick the potatoes with a fork. Put a layer of coarse salt in a baking dish and place the potatoes on top. Bake for 1 hour or until tender when pierced with the point of a knife. Remove from the oven, cut the potatoes into halves and scoop out the flesh with a spoon; mash with a potato masher until smooth.

2. Season the mashed potatoes with salt and pepper to taste, and form into small balls. Roll the balls in the flour, dip in the egg and roll in breadcrumbs; refrigerate.

3. Preheat the oven to 390°F, 200°C or gas mark 6. Ensure that the interior of the capon has been completely cleaned. Season the interior of the bird with salt, pepper and thyme; put the bay leaf into the cavity. Brush the exterior of the capon with honey, season with salt and pepper; wrap in the fig leaves.

4. Place the capon on its side in a baking dish; roast for 15 minutes, basting with the cooking juices from time to time. Insert a large fork into the cavity of the capon and turn it on to the other side; roast for another 15 minutes. Turn the capon onto its back, add about ¾ cup (200 ml) water to the roasting dish, lower the oven temperature to 320°F, 160°C or gas mark 3; continue cooking for another 25 minutes. Roasted this way, both the legs and breast of the capon will be evenly cooked.

5. Place the capon on a plate and turn it, if the juice that runs out is clear, the capon is cooked. Pour this juice into the baking dish containing the cooking liquid; stir to combine. Strain the liquid into a saucepan, skim off and discard the fat; reduce over low heat until thickened. Set the *jus* aside to keep warm.

6. Fill a large saucepan or deep fryer no more than one-third full with oil and heat to 320°F (160°C). Deep fry the croquettes in several batches until golden brown, about 2 minutes. Do not overcook.

7. Put the capon on a pretty platter and surround with the potato croquettes. Serve the *jus* in a sauceboat.

Macarons aux marrons
Chestnut Macarons

Order this dessert from your local Ladurée patisserie.

Tarte chocolat-orange
Chocolate-Orange Delight

Serves 4
Preparation: 1 hour 15 minutes
Cook: 12 minutes
Refrigerate: 3 hours
Freeze: 1 hour

Chocolate-Orange Brownie Base
7 tbsp (105 g) unsalted butter
2¾ oz (75 g) dark (65%) chocolate
2 eggs
¼ cup (50 g) superfine (caster) sugar
½ cup (60 g) all purpose (plain) flour
1¾ oz (50 g) candied orange peel, diced

Chocolate-Orange Ganache
9 oz (250 g) dark (65%) chocolate, finely chopped
½ cup + 2 tbsp (200 ml) orange juice
3½ tbsp (50 ml) heavy (double) cream
3 tbsp (45 g) unsalted butter, diced

Chocolate Glaze
5½ tbsp (80 g) heavy (double) cream
3 tbsp (45 ml) whole milk
5 tsp (20 g) superfine (caster) sugar
3½ oz (100 g) dark (65%) chocolate, finely chopped
4 tsp (20 g) unsalted butter
Candied orange peel and
chocolate truffles for decoration

Equipment
Tart (cake) ring, 8 in (20 cm) diameter, 1½ in (3 cm) high
1 candy (confectionery) thermometer

Chocolate-Orange Brownie Base
1. Melt the butter and chocolate in a bowl placed over a slowly simmering *bain-marie* (water bath); stir carefully to blend the melted ingredients. Combine the eggs and sugar and beat briskly until thick and creamy. Sift the flour and gently fold it into the egg mixture using a spatula. Add the melted butter and chocolate. Stir in the candied orange.

2. Preheat the oven to 340°F, 170°C or gas mark 3. Put the tart ring on a non-stick baking sheet and pour the brownie batter into it; bake for 12 minutes. Set aside in the ring until cold.

Chocolate-Orange Ganache
3. Put the chocolate into a bowl. Bring the orange juice and cream to the boil in a small

saucepan. Pour the boiling mixture over the chocolate. Use a rubber spatula and stir gently in small circles from the centre to the outside of the mixture to fully blend the ingredients. Check the temperature of the mixture and when it nears 122°F (50°C), stir in the butter.

4. Pour the ganache into the tart ring on top of the chocolate-orange brownie base. Refrigerate for 2 hours then, freeze for 1 hour. Slide a small knife around the inside wall of the ring to loosen and gently lift it off the brownie base and ganache; return the dessert to the freezer until required.

Chocolate Glaze

5. Put the chocolate into a bowl. Bring the cream, milk and sugar to the boil. Pour the boiling mixture over the chocolate. Add the butter and stir gently to combine the ingredients as described above.

6. Put a rack over a clean baking sheet. When the glaze is lukewarm, remove the dessert from the freezer and place it on the rack. Ladle the glaze over the dessert, completely covering it. Spread and smooth the glaze on the top and sides using a palette knife; allow it to set for at least 2 minutes. Prepare a serving plate. Slide the point of a knife between the bottom of the dessert and the rack to lift it; scrape off the excess glaze from around the edge. Carefully place the chocolate-orange delight on the serving plate. Decorate with candied orange peel and chocolate truffles. Enjoy!

Variation

This dessert can be made with a variety of other ingredients! You could make the cake batter and the ganache with red berries. For the batter, simply replace the candied orange peel with the same quantity of berries; the method and cooking time will be the same.

For a red berry ganache, use the following ingredients and the instructions outlined above:
3½ oz (100 g) raspberry puree
1¾ oz (50 g) blackcurrant puree
1¾ oz (50 g) blackberry puree
3½ tbsp (50 ml) heavy (double) cream
9 oz (250 g) dark (65%) chocolate
3 tbsp (45 g) unsalted butter.

The Art of Entertaining

Tableware
SOUP SERVICE

Soup plates, consommé bowls, soup terrine, ladle and soup spoons...whether it is a bouillon, bisque or cream of vegetable, soup has its very own service. For a slightly formal dinner, put the terrine on the table only while the soup is being served and just before the guests are seated. Traditionally, second helpings are not offered, even if the soup is delicious.

Expert Tip
SPARKLING CRYSTAL

If water has been left too long in crystal glasses and they are watermarked, fill them with warm water and add a few drops of lemon juice or white vinegar. Set aside until the marks disappear. If necessary, renew the operation. For a cloudy decanter, fill it with pure white vinegar (warmed but never hot) and coarse salt. Shake the decanter to dissolve the salt and set it aside until the solution has done its job. It may be necessary to repeat the process, at least once, to remove all marks. However, in the case of old decanters that have lost their brilliance, it is rare that they can be rejuvenated.

Savoir-Faire
WHO IS SERVED FIRST?

Traditionally, the female guest of honour is the first person to be served, followed by all the other ladies. The male guest of honour is then served, followed by the other gentlemen. The last person to be served is the host. To start eating, the hostess gives the signal, after ascertaining that everyone has been served. In less traditional settings, the hosts should establish their own protocol.

FIRESIDE SUPPER

· · ● · ·

Warm Vegetables in Vinaigrette

Pollock with Jerusalem Artichokes

Pithiviers

Spiced Fruit Macarons

· · ● · ·

Légumes confits tièdes en vinaigrette

Warm Vegetables in Vinaigrette

Serves 4
Preparation: 35 minutes
Cook: 25 minutes

4½ oz (120 g) carrots
4½ oz (120 g) salsify
4½ oz (120 g) parsley root
4½ oz (120 g) yellow turnips
4½ oz (120 g) beets (beetroot)
4 tsp (20 ml) aged red wine vinegar
3½ tbsp (50 ml) extra virgin olive oil
3½ oz (100 g) shallots, finely diced
Salt, ground white pepper
4 tsp (20 g) butter
Mesclun (mixed young salad greens)
Fleur de sel (sea salt crystals)

1. Wash, peel and cut the vegetables in to various shapes: discs, strips, triangles and small sticks. Play with their colours and shapes.
2. Prepare a bowl of chilled water and crushed ice. Cook the vegetables separately in boiling water and drain. Refresh the vegetables in the iced water to stop the cooking, drain again and set aside.
3. Put the vinegar into a small bowl, season to taste with salt and pepper and whisk to dissolve the salt. Progressively whisk in the olive oil and add the shallots.
4. Melt the butter in a pan over low heat, add the vegetables and reheat gently. Pour the vinaigrette over the vegetables. Serve in soup plates, decorate with a few leaves of mesclun and dust with *fleur de sel*. Serve immediately.

Chef's Tip

Oil and vinegar, after salt and pepper, are essential ingredients in the kitchen. However, choosing them today is certainly a challenge! A variety of oils are on the market now including, olive, walnut, sunflower... Not only that, one must consider how the oil is extracted. Is it cold pressed or extra virgin? Many types of vinegar exist too, such as wine vinegar, cider and balsamic, to name a few. Don't hesitate to experiment and combine the different flavours!

Dos de lieu jaune aux topinambours
Pollock with Jerusalem Artichokes

Serves 4
Preparation: 35 minutes
Cook: 30 minutes

---

21 oz (600 g) centre-cut pollock fillet, skin on
Salt, ground white pepper
9 oz (500 g) Jerusalem artichokes (sunchokes)
8 tsp (40 g) butter
4 tsp (20 ml) extra virgin olive oil
¼ cup (60 ml) heavy (double) cream
1 tsp (4 g) caviar
Fleur de sel (sea salt crystals)

---

1. Cut the pollock into 4 equal portions, season with salt and pepper and refrigerate.
2. Peel the Jerusalem artichokes; set half aside. Put the remainder into a saucepan, cover with cold water and season with salt. Bring the water to a slow boil and cook for 20 minutes, or until the Jerusalem artichokes are soft when pierced with the point of a knife; drain. Puree using a food mill or potato masher. Stir in 4 tsp (20 g) of the butter while the puree is still hot and season to taste with salt and pepper. Set aside to keep warm.
3. Finely slice the reserved Jerusalem artichokes. Heat the remaining butter in a frying pan, add the sliced Jerusalem artichokes and sauté; season with salt and pepper and set aside.
4. Preheat the oven to 320°F, 160°C or gas mark 3. Lightly brush a baking sheet with some of the olive oil and place the pollock on it, sprinkle with the remaining olive oil and bake for 7 minutes.
5. Bring the cream to the boil in a small saucepan and reduce until thickened; season with salt and pepper.
6. Overlap the sautéed Jerusalem artichokes to form a rosette on each plate and place a quenelle of the puree on top. Arrange the pollock skin side up on the plates with a spoonful of cream beside each portion; sprinkle with caviar and *fleur de sel*. Serve immediately.

Pithiviers
Pithiviers

Serves 6
Preparation: 1 hour
Cook: 1 hour
Rest: 9 hours 30 minutes

Puff Pastry
2 tsp (10 g) *fleur de sel* (sea salt crystals)

1 cup (250 ml) water
5 tbsp (75 g) unsalted butter
2½ cups (500 g) cake flour
14 oz (400 g) unsalted butter
Flour for the work surface

Almond Cream
7 oz (200 g) unsalted butter
1⅔ cups (200 g) confectioner's sugar
7 oz (200 g) almond flour (powder)
2½ tbsp (20 g) cornstarch (cornflour)
4 eggs
2 tbsp (30 ml) rum

Assembly
1 egg, beaten for glazing

Equipment
Cardboard
Piping bag fitted with a 3/8 in tip
Pastry brush

Puff Pastry

1. Dissolve the salt in the water. Melt the 5 tbsp (75 g) butter in a small saucepan over low heat. Sift the flour into a bowl, add the salted water and stir to combine; add the melted butter. Mix using the fingertips until all the ingredients are blended; do not overwork the dough.
2. Form the dough into a 6 in (15 cm) square, cover with plastic (cling) wrap and refrigerate for 1 hour until firm.
3. Sandwich the remaining butter between 2 sheets of baking parchment and tap with a rolling pin until softened to the same consistency as the dough. Form the butter into a square the same size as the refrigerated dough.
4. Lightly dust the work surface with flour. Remove the dough from the refrigerator and roll it out evenly to form a 12 in (30 cm) square. Place the butter diagonally in the centre of the dough. Fold the corners of the dough up and over the butter to completely enclose it in the dough; lightly tap with the rolling pin to firmly seal. (This is the *pâton*.) Roll the *pâton* out evenly into a band about 24 in (60 cm) long; fold it into thirds, carefully aligning the edges. Turn the folded dough 45° to the right and roll it out again into a band 6 in (15 cm) wide and 24 in (60 cm) long. Each time the dough is folded into thirds, it counts as 1 turn. After every second turn, wrap the dough in baking parchment and refrigerate for 2 hours. Continue, rolling and folding as described until the dough has been given a total of 6 turns. Refrigerate for a minimum of 2 hours before using or, preferably, overnight. Store the dough in the refrigerator until required.

Almond Cream

5. Cut the butter into small pieces, place in a bowl over a *bain-marie* (water bath) until soft and creamy. Remove the bowl from the bain-marie, add the following ingredients one by one, beating well after each addition:

the confectioner's sugar, almond flour, cornstarch, eggs and rum.

ASSEMBLY

6. Make two discs of cardboard; one 8½ in (22 cm) and the other 7¾ in (20 cm). Dust the work surface with flour and roll the puff pastry dough out to an even thickness of ³⁄₁₆ in (5mm). Using the cardboard discs as templates carefully cut out two discs of dough with a small knife; refrigerate the discs of dough for 2 hours.

7. Place the small disc of dough on a baking sheet. Spoon the almond cream into the piping bag. Pipe the almond cream in a spiral starting at the centre of the dough and working outwards to within ¾ in (2 cm) of the edge. Brush the exposed border of dough with cold water and cover with the large dough disc; lightly press down on the dough to seal. Use the back of a small knife to make shallow vertical indentations at ¼ in (6 mm) intervals around the side of the dough to tighten the two layers. (This is known as *chiqueter*.) Refrigerate for 30 minutes.

8. Preheat the oven to 390°F, 200°C or gas mark 6. Remove the *Pithiviers* from the refrigerator. Use the back of a small knife to trace shallow curved lines from the centre out to the edge of the dough. Brush the surface with egg glaze; do not to let it run over the sides, or the pastry will not rise correctly. Bake for 20 minutes; lower the heat to 340°F, 170°C or gas mark 3 and bake for another 40 minutes. Cool before serving.

Variation

Personalise your pithiviers: First, make the puff pastry and cut out two discs of dough. Place one on top of the other without any filling and bake as previously described. (This is known as a dry galette.) When the galette is cold, put it on a flat surface and cut it horizontally in half. Finally, spread the base with chocolate or hazelnut paste, jam or whipped cream.

...

Macarons aux épices et fruits moelleux
Spiced Fruit Macarons

Order this dessert from your Ladurée patisserie.

The Art of Entertaining

Setting the Stage

CREATE
A WINTER ATMOSPHERE

If you have a fireplace, light a fire in it and burn wood such as pine, green oak or bay laurel which contain a high percentage of resin or essential oils and which will crackle happily away.
If not, create an aromatic illusion by lighting a perfumed candle about an hour before the guests arrive. Consider using winter bouquets… Pine tree branches will conjure up the image of a winter forest and give off their perfume at the same time.

Expert Tip

WASHING CRYSTAL GLASSES

Try to avoid washing crystal glasses in the dishwasher. Or, if possible, wash a glasses-only load using special detergent on a gentle low-temperature cycle. Do not allow the glasses to touch each other in the dishwasher. The best way to wash crystal is by hand in warm, soapy water. Never use hot water because it increases the risk of breakage. Do not put several glasses in the sink at the same time; wash them one by one. Rinse and wipe dry with a lint-free cotton dish towel. If you drain the glasses on a hard work surface, place a clean, folded dish towel underneath them to reduce the risk of chipping. For hollow-stem glasses and champagne flutes clean with a long, soft bottle-brush.

Tableware

CANDLELIGHT DINNER

Candlelight makes the world appear more beautiful and warm, especially in winter. Use low candles on your table, so the flames are not at eye-level, which is very annoying. On the other hand, and for the same reason, if you use candlesticks make sure they are tall with long candles. These candles should never be scented; light them a few minutes before everyone sits down at the table.

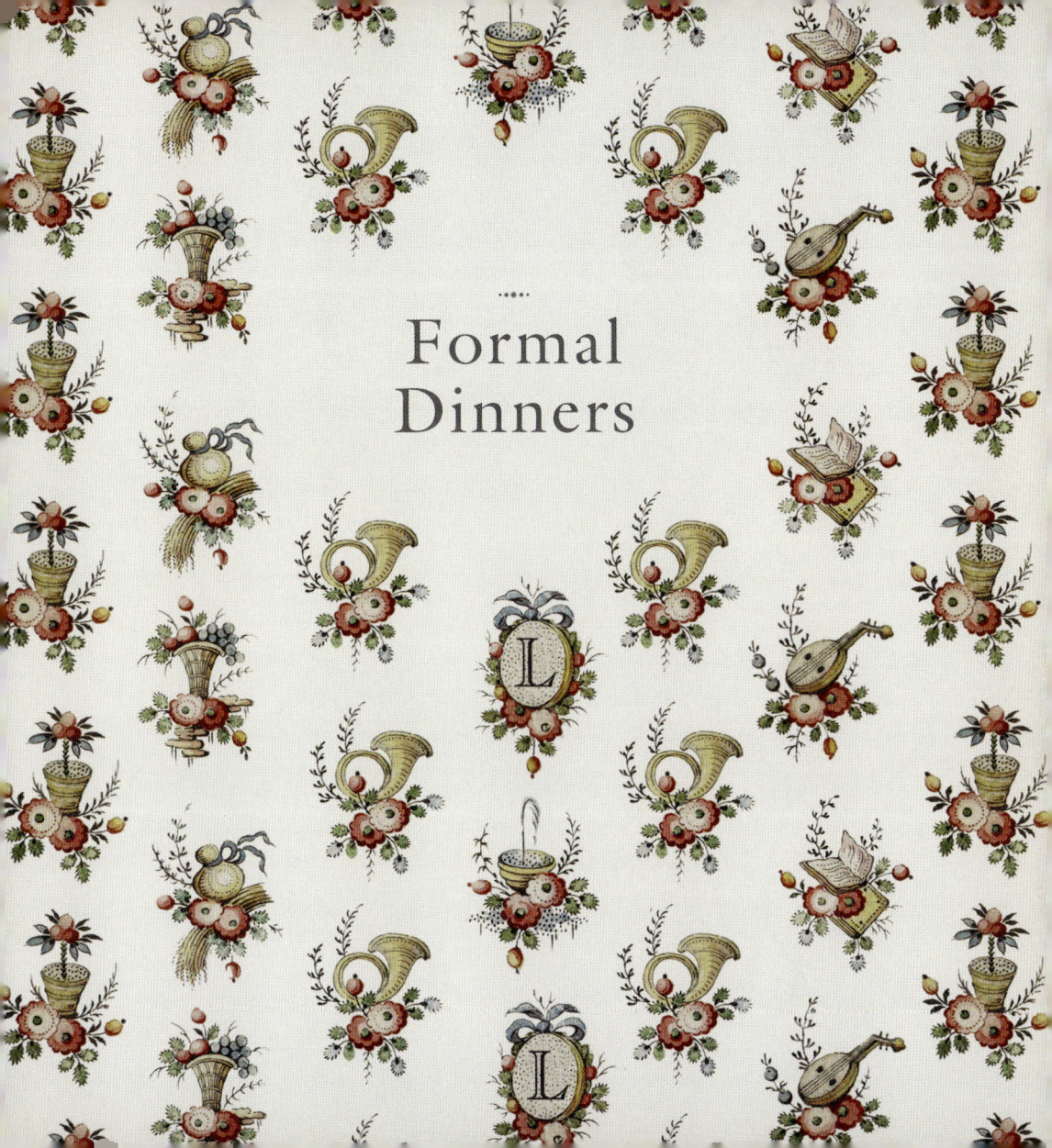

Formal Dinners

DIPLOMATIC DINNER

·•·

Foie Gras Cupcakes

Tomato-Vodka Granita with Green Vegetables

Beef with Morel Mushrooms, Potato *Madeleines*

Crispy Goat Cheese Tartlets with
Wildflower Honey

Fresh Fruit and Cream-Filled *Savarin*

Golden Chocolate Macaron *Croquembouche*

·•·

Cupcakes au foie gras landais
Foie Gras Cupcakes

Serves 8
Preparation: 35 minutes
Cook: 40 minutes
Refrigerate: 12 hours minimum

Foie Gras Cream
18 oz (500 g) fresh *foie gras*, deveined
Salt, ground white pepper
7 tbsp (100 ml) *crème fraîche*

Cupcakes
1 ⅔ cups (200 g) all purpose (plain) flour
1 scant tbsp (10 g) baking powder
4 eggs
7 oz (200 g) butter, melted
7 tbsp (100 ml) *crème fraîche*
Salt

Assembly
Fleur de sel (sea salt crystals)

Equipment
Terrine 6¼ x 4¾ in (16 x 12 cm)
Piping bag fitted with a ⅜ in (10 mm) fluted tip
8 cupcake moulds

Foie Gras Cream

1. Prepare the *foie gras* the day prior to serving. Preheat the oven to 210°F, 100°C or gas mark less than ¼. Season the *foie gras* with salt and pepper and spread it in the bottom a terrine; press firmly to smooth the surface.

2. Prepare a container of crushed ice. Fill a baking dish with hot water and put the terrine of *foie gras* into it. Transfer to the oven and cook for 20 minutes. Remove from the oven and stand the terrine in the crushed ice to cool. Refrigerate for at least 12 hours.

3. Put the *foie gras* and *crème fraîche* into the bowl of a food processor and pulse until smooth and creamy. Refrigerate.

Cupcakes

4. Preheat the oven to 355°F, 180°C or gas mark 4. Sift the flour and baking powder into a bowl and make a well in the centre. Put the eggs, melted butter, *crème fraîche* and salt into the well. Stir continuously until the batter is smooth. Fill the cupcake moulds to the ¾ mark with the batter. Bake for 15 minutes, remove from the oven and set aside until cold.

Assembly

5. Use a bread knife to slice off the tops of the cupcakes. Carefully hollow-out the centres using a small spoon. Put the *foie gras* cream into the piping bag and pipe it generously into the cupcakes. Sprinkle with *fleur de sel* and replace the tops. Enjoy!

Granité à la tomate et vodka aux légumes verts

Tomato-Vodka Granita with Green Vegetables

Serves 8
Preparation: 35 minutes
Cook: 20 minutes
Rest: 24 hoursh

---

1 lb 12 oz (800 g) tomatoes
3½ cups (800 ml) water
⅓ cup (60 g) superfine (caster) sugar
2 tbsp (30 ml) vodka
Salt, ground white pepper
5¼ oz (150 g) green beans
3½ oz (100 g) snow peas
4 asparagus tips
Fleur de sel (sea salt crystals)
2 tbsp (30 ml) extra virgin olive oil
8 sprigs chervil

---

1. Prepare the granita 24 hours before serving. Prepare a bowl of chilled water and crushed ice. Bring a saucepan of water to the boil and immerse the tomatoes for 10 seconds. Transfer immediately to the chilled water to cool; drain. Peel and quarter the tomatoes. Scoop out the pulp and seeds; set aside. Finely dice the tomato flesh; set aside.

2. Put the pulp and seeds into a food processor and process to obtain a coulis; strain using a fine mesh wire strainer. Put the coulis into a bowl, stir in the water, sugar and vodka; season to taste with salt and pepper. Pour the mixture into a shallow container and freeze for 2 hours. Remove from the freezer and stir with a fork, crushing the crystals and scraping the bottom and sides of the container so the mixture will freeze evenly. Repeat this step 4 or 5 times. Keep the granita in the freezer until required. Chill 8 small glasses or verrines.

3. On the day of serving, cook the green vegetables separately in boiling salted water, refresh in iced water; drain. Cut the green beans into small pieces and the asparagus tips lengthwise into halves. Place the green beans, snow peas and asparagus spears in a bowl and, if necessary, season again; stir gently to combine.

4. Season the diced tomato flesh with *fleur de sel* and olive oil. Divide the granita among the chilled glasses; place the diced tomato and green vegetables on top. Decorate with chervil sprigs. Serve immediately.

Chef's Tip

Granitas are often served as a palate cleanser in the middle of a multi-course meal. In this menu it is proposed as a refreshing starter. This granita would also be very pleasant served in summer.

Pavés de bœuf aux morilles et madeleines de pommes de terre

Beef Tenderloin with Morel Mushrooms, Potato Madeleines

Serves 8
Preparation: 45 minutes
Cook: 35 minutes

Potato Madeleines
14 oz (400 g) boiled and freshly crushed potatoes
3 eggs
¾ cup + 2 tbsp (200 ml) 2% (semi-skimmed) milk
1 tsp (5 g) baking powder
5½ tbsp (80 g) melted butter
Salt, ground white pepper
Softened butter for the mould

Beef Tenderloin with Morel Mushrooms
3½ oz (100 g) fresh morels
3 lbs 12 oz (1.7 kg) beef tenderloin (fillet of beef)
4 tsp (20 g) butter

Assembly
Fleur de sel (sea salt crystals)

Equipment
1 *madeleine* mould

POTATO MADELEINES
1. Heat the oven to 355°F, 180°C or gas mark 4. Put the crushed potatoes into a bowl. Beat the eggs and, little by little, stir them into the potatoes. Add the milk, baking powder and melted butter separately, stirring after each addition; season to taste with salt and pepper. Lightly brush the *madeleine* mould with softened butter. Spoon the potato mixture into the mould. Bake for 15 minutes, remove from the oven and wait for a few seconds before unmolding. Set aside to keep warm. Do not turn off the oven.

BEEF TENDERLOIN WITH MOREL MUSHROOMS
2. Rinse the morels in cold running water. Place in a saucepan of cold salted water and bring to the boil. Remove from the heat immediately, drain and set aside.
3. Trim the beef and cut it into 6 steaks; season with salt and pepper. Put the butter into a frying pan over high heat. Add the steaks and sear on both sides until lightly browned. Transfer to the oven, cook for 4 to 8 minutes, or until done as desired.
4. Pour the cooking juices from the beef into a saucepan, add the morels and cook over low heat for 6 minutes; season to taste with salt.

ASSEMBLY
5. Arrange the potato madeleines and steaks on warm plates. Garnish with morels and dust with *fleur de sel*.

Chef's Tip
If desired, prepare a beef jus with the trimmings:

Brown the trimmings in hot oil. Chop an onion, a carrot and a stick of celery. Add the vegetables and a bouquet garni to the browned trimmings, add water to cover and simmer for 30 minutes; strain. Reduce the stock to obtain a slightly syrupy jus.

Croustillants de chèvre au miel
Crispy Goat Cheese Tartlets with Wildflower Honey

Serves 8
Preparation: 20 minutes
Cook: 20 minutes

8 dried apricots
16 discs puff pastry dough, 4½ in (11 cm)
8 Saint Marcellin goat cheeses
Fleur de sel (sea salt crystals)
1 egg yolk, beaten for glazing
5 tbsp (100 g) wildflower honey

1. Preheat the oven to 355°F, 180°C or gas mark 4. Place the apricots flat on a work surface and cut each one horizontally in half. Place a puff pastry disc on a flat surface. Put an apricot half in the centre of the disc and place a goat cheese on it; top with an apricot half. Sprinkle with *fleur de sel*. Brush the exposed dough with the beaten egg and cover with a puff pastry disc; press down firmly to seal. Repeat, to make 8 tartlets.
2. Brush the surface of the tartlets with the egg glaze. Be careful not to let it run over the edges, otherwise the puff pastry will not rise evenly. Use the back of a knife to trace shallow curved lines in the shape of a flower on the top of each tartlet.
3. Cook the tartlets on a baking sheet in the oven for 20 minutes, or until golden brown. Serve warm with the honey on the side. Accompany with a green salad, if desired.

Savarin
Fresh Fruit and Cream-Filled Savarin

Order this dessert from your local Ladurée patisserie.

Pièce montée de macaron chocolat or
Gilded Chocolat Macaron Croquembouche

Order this prestigious dessert from your local Ladurée patisserie.

The Art of Entertaining

Setting the Stage

DECORATE THE ENTRANCEWAY TO YOUR HOME

An exceptional dinner requires an exceptional decor! To welcome your guests, start at the entry. Hang a small bouquet of flowers on the door handle or put up a larger garland if possible. Light outdoor candles and arrange them on the front steps. Stretch a piece of fabric above the front door to make a canopy. Show that you are delighted to receive your guests and let your decor say so.

Savoir-Faire

GIFTS FROM GUESTS

What does one do with flowers, chocolates and small gifts given by guests when they arrive? First, accompany the guests into the sitting room and make the necessary introductions. Then, put the flowers into a vase and place it appropriately in the sitting or dining room. To avoid putting the host on the spot, you can have flowers delivered with a thank you note the following morning. Or, have the flowers sent on the morning of the event. Gifts should be unwrapped and placed in the sitting room after having expressed your pleasure and appreciation for the thoughtfulness of the choices. Chocolates and other sweets could be offered after the meal, or with the coffee.

Tableware

WINE GLASSES

Usually, every place setting has two wine glasses in front of the plate. The white wine glass, the smaller of the two, is placed to the right. If a champagne flute is to be used, it is placed between the red wine and water glass, or behind the other glasses.

CELEBRATION DINNER

•••

Goat Cheese in Salmon Cannelloni

Nori-Wrapped Lobster on Bed of Lentils, Couscous and Bulgur

Veal with Truffles, Brussels Sprouts in Filo Packets

Marie-Antoinette Gâteau

White Chocolate-Coconut Truffles

•••

…

Cannellonis de saumon au chèvre frais
Goat Cheese in Salmon Cannelloni

Serves: 8
Preparation: 25 minutes

4 organic or untreated lemons
10½ oz (300 g) fresh soft goat cheese
3 tbsp chives, finely sliced
1 tsp *fleur de sel* (sea salt crystals)
¾ tsp ground white pepper
21 oz (600 g) smoked salmon, finely sliced
8 chives
4 tsp (20 ml) extra virgin olive oil

1. Zest the lemons using a fine grater. Put the goat cheese, lemon zest, chives, salt and pepper into a bowl; stir to combine. Refrigerate the cheese mixture.
2. Put a piece of plastic (cling) wrap onto a work surface and lay some smoked salmon on it to form a rectangle. Put a spoonful of the goat cheese mixture along the short side of the rectangle. Using the plastic wrap as a guide, slowly pull up the edge, and roll the salmon over forming it into a cannelloni shape. Repeat this step to make 8 cannelloni.

If desired, make large rectangles to obtain longer cannelloni and cut them into 4 in (10 cm) segments.

3. Decorate the cannelloni with chives and sprinkle with olive oil. Refrigerate before serving.

…

Homards en feuilles d'algues aux céréales
Nori Wrapped Lobster on a Bed of Lentils, Couscous and Bulgur

Serves 8
Preparation: 45 minutes
Cook: 40 minutes

Lobster
4 French lobsters, 21 oz (600 g) each
1 tbsp salt
4 tsp fresh thyme leaves
8 nori sheets

Lentils, Couscous and Bulgur
3 oz (80 g) green lentils
3 oz (80 g) onion, sliced
4½ oz (120 g) carrots, sliced
3 oz (80 g) medium grain couscous
⅔ cup water (160 ml)
3 oz (80 g) bulgur (cracked wheat)

Salt, ground white pepper

Assembly
2 tbsp (30 g) butter
4 tsp (20 ml) balsamic vinegar
Zest of 1 lime, finely grated
8 sprigs chervil
Fleur de sel (sea salt crystals)

Lobster
1. Detach the lobster claws and tails from heads. Fill a large saucepan with water; add the salt and thyme leaves. Bring to the boil, immerse the lobsters and cook the tails for 5 minutes and the claws 7 to 8 minutes; drain.
2. Shell the claws and tails. Cut the lobster tails lengthwise into halves and wrap each half in a nori sheet. Refrigerate the shelled lobster meat and wrapped tails.

Lentils, Couscous and Bulgur
3. Put the lentils, onion and carrot into a saucepan of cold water; bring to the boil. Cook the lentils over low heat. They should remain a little crunchy but be fully cooked; drain.
4. Put the couscous into a bowl. Bring 1/3 cup (80 ml) of salted water to the boil and pour it over the couscous. Cover the bowl with plastic (cling) wrap and set aside for 15 minutes, until the grains are swollen. Stir gently with a fork, taste and adjust the seasoning if necessary.
5. Prepare the bulgur as described in step 4.
6. Combine the lentils, couscous and bulgur in a bowl. Taste, and adjust the seasoning if necessary.

Assembly
7. Put the butter in a frying pan over low heat and add the claws, arms and nori-wrapped lobster; heat gently. Add the balsamic vinegar to the pan; set the pan juices aside.
8. Mound the lentil mixture on warm plates. Place a piece of wrapped lobster, a claw and an arm on each mound; drizzle with the reserved pan juices. Sprinkle with grated lime zest. Decorate with chervil sprigs and dust with *fleur de sel*.

...

Noix de veau à la truffe et bonbons de choux de Bruxelles
Veal with Truffles, Brussels Sprouts in Filo Packets

Serves 8
Preparation: 50 minutes
Cook: 25 minutes

Brussels Sprouts in Filo Packets
21 oz (600 g) Brussels sprouts

3 tbsp (45 g) butter
1 packet filo pastry
Salt, ground white pepper

Veal
8 pieces eye round (topside) veal, 6 oz (160 g) each
Salt, ground white pepper
4 tsp (20 g) butter
2 tbsp (30 ml) extra virgin olive oil

Assembly
¾ oz (20 g) black Périgord truffles, finely sliced
Fleur de sel (sea salt crystals)

BRUSSELS SPROUTS IN FILO PACKETS

1. Remove and discard the outer leaves, wash and wrap the Brussels sprouts in a damp dish (tea) towel until required.

2. Set two Brussels sprouts aside for decoration. Bring a saucepan of salted water to the boil, add the remainder and cook until tender; drain. Melt 2 tbsp (30 g) of the butter in a pan over low heat. Add the sprouts and cook until very soft, season to taste with salt and pepper; set aside until cold.

3. Melt the remaining butter. Cut the filo into 4 in (10 cm) squares. Lightly brush with the butter and place a sprout in the centre of each square. Roll the filo around it as if enclosing a candy (sweet) in a wrapper; twist the ends to seal. Refrigerate.

VEAL

4. Season the veal portions with salt and pepper. Put the butter and olive oil in a frying pan over high heat. Add the veal and cook for 3 minutes on each side, basting regularly with the pan juices.

ASSEMBLY

5. Preheat the oven to 320°F, 160°C or gas mark 3. Put the wrapped sprouts onto a baking sheet and bake for 6 minutes, or until the filo pastry is golden brown.

6. Remove the leaves from the reserved Brussels sprouts. Cut each veal portion into two pieces and place on the plates with the filo packets. Drizzle with the pan juices. Decorate with the Brussels sprouts leaves and sliced truffle; dust with *fleur de sel*.

•••

Entremets Marie-Antoinette
Marie-Antoinette Gâteau

Order this unique and prestigious dessert from your local Ladurée patisserie.

Truffes noix de coco et chocolat blanc

White Chocolate-Coconut Truffles

Makes 40
Preparation: 1 hour
Rest: 2 hours

White Chocolate Ganache
10½ oz (300 g) white chocolate
7 tbsp (100 g) coconut milk
2 tbsp (30 ml) heavy (double) cream
½ vanilla bean (pod)
7 tbsp (50 g) grated coconut

White Chocolate Coating
18 oz (500 g) white chocolate
¾ cup (80 g) grated coconut

Equipment
Piping bag fitted with a ⅜ in (10 mm) plain tip
1 candy (confectionery) thermometer

White Chocolate Ganache

1. Finely chop the chocolate on a cutting board. Melt the chopped chocolate in a bowl placed over a slowly simmering *bain-marie* (water bath). Put the coconut milk into a saucepan. Using the point of a small knife scrape the pulp from the vanilla bean into the coconut milk; bring slowly to the boil. Stir in the grated coconut and set aside to swell for 10 minutes. Pour the melted chocolate into the coconut mixture and stir well to combine the white chocolate ganache evenly.

2. Pour the ganache into a gratin dish, cover with plastic (cling) wrap and refrigerate for 1 hour until cold. Remove from the refrigerator and set the ganache aside at room temperature for 30 minutes until it is supple but still firm.

3. Spoon the ganache into the piping bag. Cover a baking sheet with baking parchment and pipe small balls of ganache onto it; refrigerate for 30 minutes to firm.

White Chocolate Coating

4. Tempering chocolate can be fairly technical. Here is a simple method: Chop the chocolate on a cutting board. Put the chopped chocolate in a bowl and melt over a slowly simmering *bain-marie* (water bath) until smooth. Pour ¾ of the chocolate onto a clean, dry work surface. Use an offset metal spatula and work the chocolate in a back and forth motion, until it starts to thicken. Return the thickened chocolate to the bowl containing the remaining melted chocolate and stir gently until evenly blended. Tempered white chocolate must be used when it is 78.8°F to 80.6°F (26 to 27°C).

Assembly

5. Remove the ganache balls from the refrigerator. Spread the grated coconut out in a flat container. Slide a fork under a ganache ball, dip it into the tempered chocolate and shake gently to remove the excess; use the fork to roll one ball at a time in the coconut. Set aside until the chocolate hardens. Refrigerate in an airtight container.

ENGAGEMENT DINNER

· • ·

Lobster-Rose Petal Carpaccio

Duck *Foie Gras*, Black Truffle Macarons

Roasted Monkfish, Green Vegetable-Mozzarella Packets

Chocolate-Blackberry Mousse Dessert

Madagascar Chocolate Mini-Tartlets

· • ·

…

Carpaccio de homard à la rose

Lobster-Rose Petal Carpaccio

Serves 8
Preparation: 35 minutes
Cook: 3 minutes

Zest of 1 organic or untreated orange
1 carrot
1 leek, green part only
1 tsp coarse salt
2 live lobsters, 21 oz (600 g) each
1 organic or untreated lime
18 rose petals
3 oz (80 g) fresh ginger, finely diced
3 tbsp (40 ml) olive oil
Arugula (rocket) leaves
Fleur de sel (sea salt crystals)
Parmesan shavings (optional)

---

1. Put the orange zest, carrot, leek green and coarse salt into a large saucepan. Fill it with water and bring to the boil.
2. Wash the lobsters in cold water. Immerse in the boiling water and cook for 2 to 3 minutes; remove and shell carefully. Set the lobster meat aside until cold. Zest the lime using a fine grater and set aside. Juice the lime. Finely slice two rose petals; set the remainder aside for decoration.
3. Finely slice the cold tail and claw meat. Overlap the slices to form rosettes on 8 plates; top with the remaining meat.
4. Sprinkle the lobster meat with lime juice and ginger. Decorate each plate with the finely sliced rose petals, 2 rose petals and arugula leaves. Drizzle with the olive oil. Dust with *fleur de sel*. Decorate with Parmesan shavings if desired. Serve immediately.

…

Foie gras de canard et son macaron à la truffe noire

Duck Foie Gras, Black Truffle Macarons

Serves 8
Preparation: 45 minutes
Cook: 20 minutes
Refrigerate: 12 hours minimum

Foie gras
18 oz (500 g) duck fresh *foie gras*, deveined

Salt, ground white pepper
3 Ladurée black truffle macarons

Black Cream
7 tbsp (100 ml) heavy (double) cream
1 tsp (4 g) squid ink
Salt, ground white pepper

Assembly
¾ oz (20 g) fresh black truffle
4 Ladurée black truffle macarons
Fleur de sel (sea salt crystals)
8 slices Ladurée kugelhopf (challah), toasted (optional)

Foie Gras

1. Prepare the *foie gras* at least 12 hours before serving. Crush the three black truffle macarons between two sheets of baking parchment; set aside. Season the *foie gras* with one teaspoon each of salt and pepper. Cut the *foie gras* lengthwise into two equal portions. Spread one portion in the bottom of a terrine and cover with a thin layer of the crushed macarons.
Put the remaining *foie gras* on top, press firmly to smooth the surface.

2. Preheat the oven to 210°F, 100°C or gas mark less than ¼. Prepare a container of crushed ice. Fill a baking dish with hot water and put the terrine of *foie gras* into it. Cook in the oven for 20 minutes. Remove from the oven and stand the terrine in the crushed ice to cool. Refrigerate for at least 12 hours.

Black Cream

3. Pour the cream into a saucepan and reduce over low heat until thickened. Stir in the squid ink, season to taste with salt and pepper; set aside to keep warm.

Assembly

4. Cut the black truffle into paper thin slices and the macarons in halves. Slice the *foie gras* into 8 equal portions. Put one slice on each plate and top with a macaron half; decorate with the sliced truffle. Spoon a ribbon of black cream around the *foie gras*; sprinkle with *fleur de sel*.

5. Accompany with toasted kugelhopf, if desired.

Chef's Tip

To cook the foie gras in a steam oven, use the following method:
Serves 8
Preparation: 45 minutes
Cook: 16 minutes
Refrigerate: 5 hours + 1 day + 6 hours + 4 days

1. *Season the foie gras with a teaspoon of salt and one of pepper. Roll in plastic (cling) wrap, forming the foie gras into an oval shape; refrigerate 5 hours. Crush 3 macarons between two sheets of baking parchment; set aside. Cut the foie gras lengthwise in halves. Spread the centre of one half with the crushed macarons and put the other half on top. Roll the foie gras tightly in several layers of plastic wrap and refrigerate for 24 hours. Preheat a steam oven to 220°F (106°C). Cook the foie gras for 8 minutes. Cool and refrigerate for 6 hours.*

2. *Cook the foie gras again as described above; cool*

and refrigerate for 4 days. The foie gras can be prepared using different flavoured macarons; use the same method.

Lotte rôtie, croustillant de légumes verts à la mozzarella et verveine

Roasted Monkfish, Green Vegetable-Mozzarella Packets

Serves 8
Preparation: 45 minutes
Cook: 20 minutes

Green Vegetable-Mozzarella Packets
2½ oz (70 g) green beans, topped and tailed
2½ oz (70 g) snow peas
7 oz (200 g) fresh fava (broad) beans
7 oz (200 g) small green peas
Salt
½ cup (50 g) fresh verbena leaves
5½ oz (150 g) mozzarella, finely sliced
8 sheets filo pastry
4 tbsp (60 g) butter, melted

Roasted Monkfish
3 lbs (1.4 kg) monkfish fillet, skinned and boned
Fleur de sel (sea salt crystals)
Ground white pepper
4 tbsp (60 g) butter

Green Vegetable-Mozzarella Packets
1. Prepare a large container of ice water. Cook the vegetables separately in boiling salted water. After cooking each vegetable, refresh immediately in the ice water to stop the cooking and then drain. Finely slice the verbena. Cut the mozzarella slices into thin strips.
2. Cover a baking sheet with baking parchment. Preheat the oven to 340°F, 170°C or gas mark 3. Spread the sheets of filo on the work surface, lightly brush with butter. Put some of the green beans in the centre of the filo and top with snow peas, verbena, fava beans, green peas and strips of mozzarella. Cover with the remaining green vegetables as previously described. Fold the sides of the filo up and over to make 4 in (10 cm) square packets; brush lightly with butter and place on the baking sheet.
3. Put the packets into the oven for 8 minutes, or until the filo is golden brown. The mozzarella will melt in the centre of vegetables without making the filo soggy.

Roasted Monkfish
4. Rinse and dry the monkfish. Cut it into 8 equal portions and season with *fleur de sel* and pepper.

5. Put the butter into a frying pan over high heat. Add the monkfish, cook for 10 minutes until golden, basting continuously. Set aside for 2 minutes before cutting each portion in half.
6. Cut each of the green vegetable packets in half and arrange on the plates; top with the monkfish. Drizzle the pan juices over the fish; sprinkle with *fleur de sel*.

Chef's Tip
Don't hesitate to ask your fishmonger to skin and bone the monkfish for you. When preparing the filo packets, put the same quantity of vegetables under and on top of the mozzarella. This way it will melt slowly without making the pastry soggy.

Entremets Vendôme
Chocolate-Blackberry Mousse Dessert

Order this prestigious dessert from your Ladurée patisserie.

Mini-tartelettes au chocolat de Madagascar
Madagascar Chocolate Mini-Tartlets

Makes 24 tartlets
Preparation: 1 hour
Cook: 20 minutes
Rest: 2 hours

Chocolate Sweet Pastry
4½ oz (120 g) cold unsalted butter
1¾ cup (200 g) cake flour
½ cup + 2 tbsp (75 g) confectioner's (icing) sugar
4 tbsp (25 g) almond powder (flour)
2½ tbsp (12 g) unsweetened cocoa powder
1 pinch *fleur de sel* (sea salt crystals)
1 egg, beaten
Softened butter for the moulds
Flour for the moulds and work surface

Madagasgar Chocolate Ganache
3½ tbsp (50 g) room temperature unsalted butter
5¼ oz (150 g) Madagasgar chocolate
⅔ cup (150 ml) heavy (double) cream

Equipment
24 mini-tartlet moulds, 1½ in (4 cm)
Piping bag fitted with a fluted tip

Chocolate Sweet Pastry

1. Cut the butter into very small pieces. Sift the flour and the confectioner's sugar separately. Put the flour into a bowl; add the butter, the confectioner's sugar, almond powder, cocoa powder and *fleur de sel*. Rub the butter into the dry ingredients with the fingertips until it resembles fine breadcrumbs. Use a wooden spoon to blend in the egg. Do not overwork the dough. Roll it into a ball, flatten and wrap in plastic (cling) wrap. Refrigerate the dough for a minimum of 1 hour before using.
2. Butter and flour the moulds. Dust the work surface with the flour. Roll the dough out evenly to a thickness of $^1/_{16}$ in (2 mm) and line the tartlet moulds with it. Refrigerate for 1 hour.
3. Preheat the oven to 340°F, 170°C or gas mark 3. Prick the dough with a fork so it will remain flat during cooking. Put the lined tartlet moulds on a baking sheet; bake for 20 minutes. Remove from the oven and set aside until the pastry is cold.

Madagasgar Chocolate Ganache

4. Cut the butter into small pieces. Finely chop the chocolate on a cutting board and put it into a large bowl. Put the cream into a saucepan and bring to the boil. Tip half the boiling cream into the chopped chocolate and whisk in a circular motion to fully blend the ingredients. Add the remaining hot cream in the same way. Stir in the butter using a spatula. Continue stirring until the ganache is smoothly blended. Set aside to cool; stir regularly.
5. Spoon the ganache into the piping bag. Pipe small rosettes of ganache into the mini-tartlets and set aside until hardened.

Chef's Tip

If you wish, use other types of chocolate such as those from Columbia, Ghana or Ecuador.

The Art of Entertaining

A Touch of Madness

HIRE A BUTLER FOR THE EVENING

When holding a gala dinner, consider hiring a butler, or even the services of a team who will take over your kitchen, cook, serve and clean-up. This way, you will have the opportunity to relax and, at the same time, feel like a guest in your own home! There are all types of personnel available for in-house occasions, it simply depends on what you feel is appropriate and necessary.

Tableware

BEAUTIFUL SERVING DISHES AND ACCESSORIES

There is an appropriate serving dish for every course: round and shallow plates for hors-d'oeuvres, cold vegetables or desserts; round and flat plates for savoury or sweet tarts and cakes, oval platters for fish and meat; and covered dishes to keep vegetables warm. Specific tableware has been created for asparagus, oysters, artichokes, snails, caviar and even devilled eggs (which used to be very popular...). Use utensils such as sauce spoons, asparagus tongs, cake and tart servers, pastry tongs and pickle forks.

An Expert Tip

KEEP A NOTE BOOK WITH GUEST DETAILS

Note everything you need to remember concerning your guests' food preferences, allergies, the names of people to whom you have introduced them, and those who have already been invited to your home.
Mark the dates of each event and gifts received; include other more personal details such as children's names, usual vacation locations... The easiest way to do this is to keep all the names in alphabetical order, in a small thumb-index note book.

Recipe Index

SAVOURY

Starters

- P. 204 Choux Puffs with Eggplant Caviar and Kalamata Olives
- P. 236 Country-Style Duck Pâtés in Puff Pastry
- P. 244 Cream of Red Hubbard Squash and Almond Soup
- P. 288 Duck *Foie Gras*, Black Truffle Macarons
- P. 214 Duck *Foie Gras* on a Bed of Cherries
- P. 76   *Foie Gras* and Truffle Terrine
- P. 268 *Foie Gras* Cupcakes
- P. 128 Garden Pea and Mint Gaspacho
- P. 222 Goose *Foie Gras* Dressed in Red and Black
- P. 108 Langoustine Carpaccio with Ginger
- P. 86   Lavender and Avocado *Éclairs*
- P. 214 Lobster-Rose Petal Carpaccio
- P. 98   Pork and Veal Pâté in a Pastry Crust
- P. 59   Salmon Marinated with Cardamom and Mint
- P. 224 Sea Bass Tartar with Pink Grapefruit
- P. 64   Smoked Salmon with Citrus Caviar
- P. 270 Tomato-Vodka Granita with Green Vegetables
- P. 77   Vegetable Gaspacho
- P. 254 Warm Vegetables in Vinaigrette
- P. 120 Wild Mushroom *Religieuses*

Fish and Shellfish

- P. 205 Crab-Filled Avocado Cannelloni
- P. 278 Goat Cheese in Salmon Cannelloni
- P. 206 John Dory Fillets with Apples and Jasmine Cream
- P. 288 Lobster-Rose Petal Carpaccio
- P. 278 Nori Wrapped Lobster on a Bed of Lentils, Couscous and Bulgur
- P. 238 Pike-Perch with Grape-Red Wine Preserves and Forgotten Vegetables
- P. 258 Pollock with Jerusalem Artichokes
- P. 130 Red Mullet, Carrots and Strawberries
- P. 291 Roasted Monkfish, Green Vegetable-Mozzarella Packets
- P. 89   Salmon Loaf
- P. 172 Vegetable Gratin, Jumbo Shrimp Brochettes

Meat and Poultry

- P. 110 Beef Tenderloin, Vitelotte Potato Purée and Chips, Candied Violets
- P. 272 Beef Tenderloin with Morel Mushrooms, Potato *Madeleines*
- P. 215 Duck Breast, Pistachio Polenta "Fries"
- P. 244 Honeyed Capon in Fig Leaves, Potato Croquettes
- P. 122 Lamb Shanks with Vanilla, Apple Compote
- P. 195 Steak and Caper Tartar, Gaufrette Potatoes
- P. 280 Veal with Truffles, Brussels Sprouts in Filo Packets
- P. 224 Veal with Truffle Ravioli
- P. 188 Veal *Piccata*, Lemony Orzo Risotto

Vegetarian

- P. 184 Cheese Soufflé
- P. 273 Crispy Goat Cheese Tartlets with Wildflower Honey
- P. 32 *Fromage Blanc* with Fresh Herbs
- P. 16 Melun Brie Cheese with Almonds
- P. 185 Mushroom Tartlets
- P. 48 Parisian Brioches Filled with Creamy Green Vegetables
- P. 172 Salty Ladurée Kisses
- P. 194 Tomato *Mont-Blanc*
- P. 182 Vegetable Ravioli, Kaffir Lime Cream
- P. 96 Vegetable Terrine, Fresh Tomato Sauce

Eggs

- P. 32 Baked Eggs with Cream
- P. 58 Baked Goose Eggs, Tomato Compote
- P. 12 Concorde Omelette
- P. 96 Devilled Goose Eggs
- P. 15 Poached Eggs with Bacon
- P. 46 Poached Eggs on Toast with Morel Mushrooms
- P. 24 Scrambled Eggs with Sea Urchin Roe
- P. 24 Soft-Boiled Eggs with Black Truffle
- P. 66 Truffle Omelette

Sandwiches

- P. 64   Chicken, Cucumber and *Fromage Frais* Finger Sandwiches
- P. 16   Herbed *Fromage Blanc* Finger Sandwiches
- P. 77   Lobster Mini-Club Sandwiches
- P. 44   Pastrami Club Sandwich
- P. 100   Pistachio-Sour Cherry Club Sandwiches
- P. 56   "Surprise" Bread

Salads

- P. 194   Lobster, Roasted Squash Seeds and Salanova Salad
- P. 88   Raw Vegetable Basket
- P. 174   Regal Salad
- P. 185   Smoked Organic Salmon and Salsola Salad

DESSERTS

Large Cakes and Tarts

- P. 227   A Citrus Heart to Share
- P. 292   Chocolate-Blackberry Mousse Dessert
- P. 247   Chocolate-Orange Delight
- P. 273   Fresh Fruit and Cream-Filled *Savarin*
- P. 59   Fruit Loaf Cake
- P. 273   Gilded Chocolat Macaron *Croquembouche*
- P. 49   Gingerbread
- P. 48   Kugelhopf with Pink Candied (Sugared) Almonds
- P. 92   Lemon Meringue Tart
- P. 131   Lemon Verbena Cream and Peach Tart
- P. 189   Linzertorte
- P. 281   *Marie-Antoinette Gâteau*
- P. 142   Minted Red Fruit Charlotte
- P. 258   *Pithiviers*
- P. 67   Rose Loaf Cake
- P. 189   *Saint-Honoré Gâteau*

Small Cakes and Tartlets

- P. 17   Black Fig Turnovers
- P. 247   Chestnut Macarons
- P. 36   Chocolate Butter on Toast

P. 216	Chocolate Cat's Tongues	P. 145	Sour Cherry and Almond Ice Cream
P. 152	Chocolate *Financiers*		
P. 35	Citrus-Almond Bostocks		**Drinks and Sweetmeats**
P. 28	French Toast and Apricot Compote	P. 160	Chocolate-Orange Cream
P. 155	Hazelnut- Cinnamon Shortbreads	P. 102	Rose and Coconut Meringues
P. 176	Lime-Basil *Éclairs*	P. 156	Rose and Vanilla Chantilly Creams
P. 292	Madagascar Chocolate Mini-Tartlets	P. 140	Rose Milkshakes
P. 198	Melon Macarons	P. 210	Rose Nougat
P. 80	Mint-Aniseed Macarons	P. 92	Rose, Violet and Jasmine White Chocolate *Tuiles*
P. 178	Minted Strawberry Macarons		
P. 111	Orange Blossom *Religieuses*	P. 230	Soft Chocolate-Macadamia Caramels
P. 190	Orange-Passion Fruit Macarons	P. 152	Viennese Coffee
P. 66	Pearl Sugar Brioches	P. 284	White Chocolate-Coconut Truffles
P. 160	Raspberry-Chocolate Tartlets		
P. 260	Spiced Fruit Macarons		**Fruity Desserts**
P. 60	Spiced Mango *Tatin* Tartlets	P. 17	Apple-Rhubarb Compote
P. 78	Strawberry-Rhubarb Cupcakes	P. 239	Caramelised Autumn Fruit, Spiced *Arlettes*
P. 196	Wild Strawberry Tartlets	P. 34	Fresh Fruit Salad
		P. 26	*Fromage Blanc* and Raspberries
	Ice Creams and Sorbets	P. 208	Kirsch-Flamed Cherries, Pistachio Ice Cream
P. 218	Lemon *Vacherin* with Candied Lemons	P. 124	Passion Fruit-Coconut Mousse Verrines
P. 198	Mascarpone Sorbet	P. 175	Strawberries in Rosé Wine Soup
P. 164	Melon Sorbet		

Guest Book

GUEST BOOK

GUEST BOOK

GUEST BOOK

GUEST BOOK

GUEST BOOK

GUEST BOOK

GUEST BOOK

GUEST BOOK

Vincent Lemains

Pastry Chef

In April 2011 Vincent Lemains joined the prestigious Ladurée establishment as Pastry Chef, responsible for patisserie creations. Twice a year, in harmony with the seasons and the Paris *haute couture* fashion shows, he envisions new flavours and colours for the French pastry classics such as the *Religieuse*, the *Saint-Honoré* and, of course, the macarons for which Ladurée is famous. These marvellous creations can be found around the world in every Ladurée boutique, where excellence and beauty are constant rivals.

Michel Lerouet

Executive Head Chef

Ladurée's Executive Head Chef is Michel Lerouet. Chef Lerouet is responsible for both the French and international kitchens. In his cuisine, what he loves and strives for are dishes with measured rhythms which slowly come to the fore, where flavours develop progressively, without dominating the palette. Michel Lerouet continuously gives the very best of himself, applying all his *savoir faire* and determination to ensure product quality in keeping with Ladurée's image.

Acknowledgements

Vincent Lemains thanks Antoine Bled for his assistance in the development and realisation of the patisserie creations. Chef Lemains also thanks the heads of the Patisserie, Chocolate and Macaron Departments: Bertrand Bernier, Julien Christophe and Franck Lenoir.

Michel Lerouet thanks his assistant Jimmy Elisabeth, as well as Marianne Delille, Aurélie Ganet, Christophe Mirta, Stéphane Renaud, Yohann Marraccini, Steeve Ildevert, Nicolas Gay, Jean-Pierre Rawotea, Vincent Gadaud and Arnaud Vautier.

Ladurée thanks Hanako Schiano, Agathe Bicart-Sée, Nastasia Brzezinski of the Communication and Marketing Department, Marie-Pierre Morel and Minako Norimatsu for their beautiful work, as well as Lionel Guerpillon of the Hôtel de l'Abbaye and Au vert et + for the sumptuous flowers found throughout Ladurée's premises.

Styling Accessories

·····

Selfish Breakfast: Platter—Christofle
Romantic Breakfast: Platter—Mis En Demeure / Flowers—Lachaume
Family Breakfast: Plate—Au Bain Marie / Flowers—Lachaume
Elegant Brunch: Name card—Ladurée
Eccentric Brunch: Plates—Fornassetti / Glasses—Mis En Demeure
Hint of Spring Brunch: Plates—Yves Halard / Glasses and vase—Mis En Demeure / Radish knife-holders, ceramic butterfly, birds and goblets—Les Fées / Flowers—Sol y Flor
Idyllic Picnic: Paper plate, 'religious' serviette—Ladurée / Paper cup—Caspari
Colourful Picnic: Picnic basket and rug (left)—Old England / Panther napkin (serviette) and invitation—Caspari / Dish towel and tablecloth—Les Toiles du Soleil
Vibrant Picnic: Tablecloth and napkin (serviette) — Les Toiles du Soleil / Square and rectangular plates—Caspari / Plates, goblets, wine glass—Tsé Tsé / Murano glass—Christophe d'Aboville

Lunch in the Garden: Bowl and pitcher (used as a vase)—Au Bain Marie / Place card—Caspari / Flowers—Lachaume
Sunday Lunch: Statuette—Cire Trudon / Butter dish, glasses, coral and plates—Mis En Demeure / Bread basket—Au Bain Marie / Cutlery—Christofle / Flowers—Lachaume
Spring Lunch: Dragonfly and butterfly plate—Les Fées / Plate, bowls and glasses (golden glazed interiors)— Tsé-Tsé / Napkin (serviette) —Les Toiles du Soleil / Flowers—Sol y Flor
A Touch of Rose: Placemat—Christophe d'Aboville / Candle—Ladurée / Napkin (serviette) —Noël / Timbale—Au Bain Marie / Flowers—Sol y Flor
Delicious Morsels: Tea pot, creamer and sugar bowl—Au Bain Marie / Napkin (Serviette)—Noël / Flowers—Lachaume
Essentially Chocolate: Name card holder—Au Bain Marie / Silver flatware—Christofle
Summer Evening Buffet: Glasses and goblets—Saint Louis / Candle—Cire Trudon
Autumn Sunset Buffet: Plates—Hermès / Glasses—Saint Louis / Jug used as a vase—Mis en Demeure Antiquité / Napkins (Serviettes)—Alexandre Turpault / Flowers—Lachaume

Published in 2021 by The Rosen Publishing Group, Inc.
29 East 21st Street, New York, NY 10010

Copyright © 2021 by The Rosen Publishing Group, Inc.

First Edition

All rights reserved. No part of this book may be reproduced in any form without permission in writing from the publisher, except by a reviewer.

Editor: Siyavush Saidian
Book Design: Reann Nye

Photo Credits: Cover Photo by Mike Kline (notkalvin)/Momnet/Getty Images; Series Art PinkPueblo/Shutterstock.com; p. 5 Pham Le Huong Son/Moment/Getty Images; p. 7 DanielBendjy/E+/Getty Imgaes; p. 9 CHBD/iStock/Getty Images Plus/Getty IMages; p. 10 aerogondo2/Shutterstock.com; p. 13 bakdc/Shutterstock.com; p. 15 mrmohock/Shutterstock.com; pp. 16–17 Joe Raedle/ Hulton Archive/Getty Images; p. 19 Chris Ryan/ OJO Images/Getty Images; p. 21 Bloomberg Creative Photos/Getty Images; pp. 23, 41 Bettmann/Getty Images; p. 24 https://commons.wikimedia.org/wiki/File:Unitedstatesreports.jpg; p. 25 https://commons.wikimedia.org/wiki/File:Alabama_v._North_Carolina,_560_U.S._(2010)_slip_opinion.pdf; p. 27 The Washington Post/Getty Images; p. 28 Chip Somodevilla/ Getty Images News/Getty Images; p. 31 Robert Alexander/ Archive Photos/Getty Images; p. 33 f11photo/Shutterstock.com; pp.34–35 OLIVIER DOULIERY/AFP/Getty Images; p. 37 Chip Somodevilla/Getty Images News/Getty Images; p. 39 Bloomberg/Getty Images; p. 40 Mark Wilson/Getty Images News/Getty Images; p. 43 Win McNamee/Getty Images News/Getty Images; p. 45 Bill Ross/The Image Bank/Getty Images.

Library of Congress Cataloging-in-Publication Data

Names: Tolli, Jenna, author.
Title: Inside the Supreme Court / Jenna Tolli.
Description: New York : Rosen Publishing, 2021. | Series: Rosen verified: U.S government | Includes index.
Identifiers: LCCN 2020005115 | ISBN 9781499468649 (library binding) | ISBN 9781499468632 (paperback)
Subjects: LCSH: United States. Supreme Court–Juvenile literature.
Classification: LCC KF8742 .T65 2021 | DDC 347.73/26-dc23
LC record available at https://lccn.loc.gov/2020005115

Manufactured in the United States of America

Some of the images in this book illustrate individuals who are models. The depictions do not imply actual situations or events.

CPSIA Compliance Information: Batch #BSR20. For Further Information contact Rosen Publishing, New York, New York at 1-800-237-9932.